Your
Secret
Self

Also by Earl Koile
Listening As a Way of Becoming

your Secret Self

earl koile

Calibre

Calibre Books/a division of Word Books, Publisher
Waco, Texas

ISBN 0-8499-0065-4
Library of Congress catalog card number: 77-92456
Printed in the United States of America

To Keith Miller,
whose seasoned friendship stays fresh and new

Contents

Preface and
Acknowledgments

Elusive and often mysterious emotions pervade our personalities and influence our behavior; they inhabit our bodies, to use Theodor Reik's term, like "hidden roomers." They cloud self-understanding, fragment our sense of wholeness, and distort our views of other people. Lacking awareness of many of our feelings, we become emotionally impoverished and out of touch with our deeper human desires and needs.

When feeling emotionally lost or troubled—conflicted, worried, anxious—we can turn to our secret ally in the strength that lies deeply within us. But in order to discover and release this strength, we must first get beneath the defensive overlays and learn to sort out the mixes and the meaning of our emotions. In the pages that follow, the experiences of many people who struggle—often successfully, sometimes not—to reach beyond their defenses to their strength are described and explored.

This book is a sequel to my last one, *Listening as a Way of Becoming*, in the sense that emphasis throughout both is on listening. Here, however, more emphasis is placed on what happens and what we can discover when we are heard, along with demonstrations of ways we listen to ourselves and others. A major focus is on finding and using the strength in our deeper emotions—those we openly acknowledge, those that elude us, and those we hold secret.

As in my last book, people with whom I have worked and lived are collaborators in this work. They include members of my family; students; colleagues; persons with whom I have worked in counseling and psychotherapy, in training, and in a host of special workshops and institutes. The anecdotes presented are based on recordings, written reports from the people involved, notes written following particular incidents, and condensations of logs I have kept of personal and professional events. Anecdotes are used with permission from the individuals portrayed; their names have been changed to provide privacy.

I want to express gratefulness and admiration for some of the people who helped in the writing of this book and who often made it personally pleasurable and intellectually stimulating. I am indebted to my students, who often turn out to be *my teachers* about the ways we learn and the ways we stifle learning. I want to pay tribute to the people with whom I work in psychotherapeutic experiences, for they often show a seasoned wisdom about our human strengths and frailties and about the fruits and failures of our uses of one another as we reach for larger purposes and deeper measures of richness in living.

12

My wife, Carmon, offered sensitive and creative suggestions throughout my work and writing. Marjorie Menefee, friend and colleague, examined this work with the perspective of a trained and experienced clinician and the patience of a sensitive and compassionate reader. Keith Miller, friend and colleague through the years, has continued to be both a wise critic and a tireless booster.

Cathy Leary, former student and now a colleague, shared personal experiences, professional insights, and delightfully infectious attitudes. Anna Marie Gonzáles, as a Ph.D. student and as a colleague who, on occasion, joined me as cotherapist, read the manuscript and enlivened some of the pages for me by adding from her own rich experiences. Chris Chavez typed parts of the manuscript; she also read it with an uncluttered freshness that is uniquely hers. Cathy Hubbard generously helped to get the final work typed, reproduced, and, finally, in the mail.

Nevitt Sanford, an eminent psychologist and the founder and President of The Wright Institute, has been in the wings for me during much of my college teaching. Through his well-known research and writing, his innovative thinking about higher education, and his ways of understanding students, he has exemplified what it means to be intellectually alive and growing and a vital force in the lives of countless people.

My acknowledgements would be incomplete without saying that Pat Wienandt, my editor at Word Books, with her sharp skills and gentle ways, has provided a warm and supportive climate for completing this work. I feel especially keen appreciation for her.

1. Emotional Controls And Cover-Ups

I was having lunch with a friend, and in the middle of our conversation he abruptly changed the subject. "You know," he said, "I'm so sick and tired of growing, of trying to change, I mean working on my own personal growth." He paused and then added, "Right now I don't want to raise a hand to understand myself any better." After another few seconds he went on, "It's not that I've changed that much. I'm just tired of trying so hard." There was a genuine push-pull feeling, a need to give up and quit working and yet a need to hold on and keep trying. I recognized those feelings, for I experience them often.

EXCESSIVE SELF-CONTROLS

I work hard sometimes to understand myself. I also work hard not to. Sometimes I get glimpses of this yes-no conflict within me. When stuck in a bothersome situation I may discover that I have gone blind to my options, gotten locked into a rigid way of thinking, or shut out emotions that I need to feel more fully if I am to break loose and change.

Why I hide some of my emotions may not always be difficult to understand. I may disown them out of fear that they are inconsistent with the person I am or want to be. I may fear what other people will think if they know too much about what I am like. This concern may be realistic; someone may indeed reject me or think less favorably of me. I may fear that if I try to change in some important way, I might fail and feel hopeless. I may choose then to fail a little every day, almost unnoticed, by living in the same ruts, rather than to try new behavior and risk failing more obviously.

Sometimes I attribute my inability to manage my life differently to the expectations, social norms, and values of others. Excessive control over my actions may be a major deterrent to my own self understanding, since it may lead me to become inflexible and impermeable. A chink in my armor, however, may reveal hidden feelings in other forms—anxiety, anger, depression, loss of humor and spontaneity, lack of energy, or other physical reactions, to name a few.

LETTING GO, DISCOVERING CHANGE

An experience with Sally, a bright, ambitious college senior, illustrates some of the consequences of shackling ourselves and of relinquishing such inordinate constraints. Those among us who knew Sally saw her as competent, fairly autonomous, stimulating in conversation, and certain to achieve. Underneath she felt scared, inadequate, sometimes helpless. Her intense efforts to present herself as flawless were sapping her energy. She responded to new and potentially threatening situations by excessive control of her feelings and actions. She feared that if she let go and trusted her deeper feelings that she would be helpless, unlovable, and rejected. The discrepancy between her increasing self-demands and her inability to meet them had become too much to manage. Finally, in desperation and on the edge of an emotional breakdown, she sought help.

After several therapy sessions Sally gradually became able to relax some of the psychological vigilance over her life; she became less concerned about what she and others might think if, for example, she did not make straight A's and did not always say and do the "right things." She discovered some intriguing paradoxes about herself. As she relinquished a few constraints over her life she began to change and then to discover the changes, rather than the other way around—to work directly to force change, fail, feel a loss of self-influence, and then tighten the controls to improve her life situation.

Minor examples of Sally's changes and her discovery of them illustrate what happened. She was unusually shy around young men, and went to great lengths to avoid being conspicuous in their presence. Then one day she said, "Last night I walked to the dorm, and before realizing it, I had walked through a group of men standing there talking on the steps. And do you know what? I not only walked right through, I nodded to them. They nodded to me in the most friendly way, as though it were the most natural thing in the world."

Then she added, "I've never done that. I usually walk around to the back door to avoid them. Wonder how I happened to walk to that front door?" She described other surprising changes that had been occurring. They were surprising in that she was discovering them as they happened rather than making them happen. For example, while hearing other people

17

talk about things they were doing, she could now say to herself, "I can do that," rather than her usual, "I could never do that at all." These changes in Sally did not constitute what you might call a major personality reorganization, but they were important steps that signaled new directions in her feelings about herself.

In letting go of some of the self-demands in pursuit of perfection, Sally discovered that she did not become helpless. Still, she had to risk such a possibility; there were no guarantees. Having taken the risk, however, she found that her venturesome attitudes toward day-to-day activities were building up momentum. She was becoming more spontaneous and aware of feelings that had been previously hidden. And she was finding a great deal of pleasure and hope in what was happening.

Sally was surprised also to discover just how unrelenting she had been in her self-domination. She had thought she was simply exercising self-discipline. She now began to learn to strike a balance between self-discipline and self-expression, a balance that released her from her own brand of despotism.

Can you recall instances in which you changed and then discovered it? And on the other side, can you recall deliberate, driving, almost unrelenting efforts to change something within yourself, only to discover that you failed, that no change occurred? I am not suggesting that we can always rely on change to slip up on us while we sit idly by to wait and watch. I am suggesting that at times there are ways we can give up some of our watchdog behavior that keeps us rigid, and ways we can become more open and responsive to ourselves and our life situations.

At such times, in letting go of some of the rigidity, we may begin to feel hope that we can change, that we can feel differently. As I relax my vigilance I become more willing to risk trying new behavior and more able to be with others in new ways. Yet, the risks seem less overwhelming, more natural. The consequences of what I do seem less catastrophic; I seem to have more freedom to fail and to believe that I will survive. Occasionally I may not know the origin or causes of my feelings of hope or of the initial spark for openness to change. Once the spark is struck, however, self-defeating cycles may be turned into enhancing upward swings.

CONTROLLING, FEELING CONTROLLED

In some of our relationships we may try to get what we need from others by attempting to control and to change them. Or we may feel controlled; to some extent we actually may be controlled. In a marriage, for example, the decision made by one partner to leave the marriage changes the relationship, even though the rebuffed partner wants to keep the marriage intact. The long and agonizing process by which the decision was born may have been kept secret by the discontented spouse. The other partner then may persist in the belief that he or she can change the decision and alter the course of events that are to follow. It is terribly difficult for us to acknowledge that we can do little or nothing about some decisions made by others that drastically alter our lives. To protect ourselves we may keep reality from our door and act as though we do have a choice in the matter. *Moreover, we may have to go through some painful experiences to assimilate the decision or to make it ours too in order to retain a feeling of influence over ourselves and our relationships.*

Sheila was a thirty-three-year old teacher whose husband had left her after ten years of marriage. He moved to another city and announced that he would file for divorce within six months. She could file

19

sooner if she wished, but his mind was made up; he would not stay married. During counseling sessions Sheila explored painstakingly all the possible causes of his leaving. She planned ways she could change his mind, what she could do to get him back, and ways she could change to please him. At the same time, Sheila was not certain that she wanted to please him or that she wanted him back. He had been extremely critical of her for years.

She began to explore whether or not *she* wanted to stay married. She did not like living with her husband; she did not feel love or loved; she knew that he meant it when he said he would file within six months if she did not file sooner. Looking only at the facts, her debate about staying married was unreal. The decision had been made, and she could not change it. Still, she needed to act as if she had influence over the decision. Her anxiety was building; it could become unbearable if she let herself face fully at this time the reality that the decision was out of her hands.

As Sheila both grasped for a marriage that had ended and searched for ways to cope with its dissolution, she continued to go over the pros and cons of it in a somewhat ritualistic manner. She tried to cover up her feelings of pain and fragility. She needed to be heard sensitively and compassionately; she needed not to be criticized (she was an expert in inviting and getting criticism) or to have the harsh realities hammered into her head. She especially needed help in finding areas of hope in her life and in realizing that her tenacity could serve as a strength. She needed hope in believing that she was lovable or could become so.

As she slowly became able to withstand the pain and to reduce her feelings of rejection, she felt less afraid of the shadowy upheavals that divorce could bring to her life. When she could see promise of survival—after discovering that she wanted to survive—and could feel hope for a future, she could give up the almost secret delusion that she alone was faced with making a decision about her marriage. She could recognize the fact that a decision had been made by her husband. *More importantly, she learned that she had to make a parallel decision of her own for dissolution of the marriage, and that her decision, as well as his, gave force, validity, and finality to their parting, and also restored her sense of influence over her life.*

Nevertheless, for awhile still, Sheila needed to allow some of the hurt, anger, and grief from this disturbing experience to remain hidden. Later, before these feelings became corrosive from being held within too long, it is to be hoped she would let them out in a way suitable for her.

Another incident, quite different, also illustrates how we lose perspective on a relationship and our desire or ability to change it. Bill, in his early fifties, and his son, twenty-three, had a huge conflict that left each feeling anger toward himself and the other. To establish a separate identity from his father, Bill's son, possibly in revenge, or perhaps for other reasons, changed his last name, taking his mother's family name and giving up his father's. Bill felt anger, wounded pride, and a sense of loss. He railed against his son and himself. Finally, after expressing all these feelings, Bill said, "I just can't accept it, and I can't get over it."

His therapist, after a short pause, replied softly but firmly, "But there is nothing that you can do about that so far as he is concerned. You cannot change his name, and you cannot make him change it." Bill repeated the words slowly as though talking to himself to let the words soak in. "There's nothing I can do about that. Nothing." He then looked up with a smile of relief and added, "Well, I'll be damned. I really can't change that!"

21

This fairly obvious observation had not occurred to him before in quite this way. He had held onto the belief that he had to continue to try to change a situation that was beyond his control. The son did not change his name back; neither did Bill forgive him immediately. What did happen was that Bill slowly began to get accustomed to the fact that his son had another name. He quit punishing himself and conjuring up revenge fantasies against his son for the fight they had, and after several months he decided to reestablish contact. But this could happen only after he had first given up the notion that he could control his son and the belief that the name change was a lifetime barrier to a relationship between the two of them. They have begun to establish an amiable although cautious relationship, each with a separate identity.

The need to control other people so that they will conform to our needs and expectations is difficult to give up. But in attempting to impose such constraints, we hamper our own ability to change and limit the flexibility, range, and diversity of how we can be with them. We also suffer a loss of influence over ourselves and other people.

WHAT HELPS YOU CHANGE?

If you do not change in ways you wish, carry out your New Year's resolutions, whom do you blame? Do you suspect that the reasons lie within? Or do you believe that they rest with others, with your "life circumstances?" On the other side, whom do you credit when you take steps forward in improving your life? Yourself? Others? Luck? We may have characteristic ways of accounting for our successes and failures to live happily, change ourselves, or break habits—quit smoking, work more, work less, act more kindly, patiently, or lovingly toward others.

Of importance here is to tease out what, or whom, we regard as having influence over our behavior. Conceivably we can get into the trap of believing that it is always completely up to us as individuals, or that it is completely in the hands of other people and life around us. Or, secretly, if not openly, we may believe that we cannot change. "You can't change human nature!"

There is plenty of research evidence, as well as instances in our daily lives, to dispute the claim that people cannot change.[1] Yet we could find ourselves living out the fact of being unable to change by staying in the same environment with the same people doing the same things daily, and becoming completely, and perhaps boringly, predictable—and unchangeable. Our anxiety may be reduced by knowing what our lives will be like each day, but so may the quality of our living.

We need to learn to uproot ourselves a bit in our relationships with other people and in choosing our environment. We can do this by seeking and creating new relationships, new situations, new environments, new experiences. Out of our need for new perspectives we take trips and vacations to vary our life routines; we enter upon new careers; we try out different life styles; we enter different kinds of groups for new and intensive experiences. In the extreme, a few among us "leave it all behind" and head for Australia or some other new and distant place for a new start in life and on our lives. And some of us remain at home and daydream about leaving.

Sanctions from Others

To let others know how we have changed—the new feelings we have acquired, the different beliefs we have formed, the life-changing decisions we have

23

made—and to have those changes sanctioned helps us to stabilize them and build them into our public image.[2] I have felt the power of such support from incidents in my life. The greater the likelihood of being sanctioned by others, the easier it is to acknowledge the changes we want to build into our self-picture. Decisions to go to college, for example, usually are sanctioned—education is good—and, therefore, easily made public.

Decisions or life-style changes that go against prevailing social norms, however, are more difficult to make public and to integrate as a stable part of our self-image. We face the prospect of disapproval when we openly demonstrate such attitudes and behavior. Before going public we may need to try out behavior changes in private for awhile—like trying on new clothes in the privacy of the fitting room before walking into public view for outside appraisal.

Decisions to divorce still go against the social grain, and often are held secret until public acknowledgment is necessary. Some individuals with whom I consult seem to withhold from themselves for extended periods of time the decision to leave their spouse—eventually. It is as though they have decided deeply within themselves that the marriage has ended, but cannot yet face from themselves and others the condemnation, guilt, and other disturbing effects. Some individuals appear to have withheld from themselves for years the inner knowledge that their marriages have irreparably failed. They may continue routines of living a married life after the relationship has died.

Once we make difficult decisions known to ourselves and then known publicly, we may find disapproval in many forms, but we also may find a surprising degree of support, often from people who have experienced similar conflicts and change. If we find no support, it may be because we ourselves have not come to terms with our actions. We may be withholding support from ourselves and at the same time disallowing or failing to recognize the support genuinely given by others.

Using a Crisis

A crisis may lead to important decisions and changes. Dealing with crisis may enable us to find new strength and to define our limits more clearly or bring out new and hidden sides of our personalities. Some of us may wait for a crisis to change our lives; we may want to turn ourselves over to larger destiny, a more powerful fate. We might then feel less responsible for what happens to us and for what we do. Others among us may secretly seek or wish for a crisis to intervene in our lives. It is not unusual for a spouse to fantasize, perhaps fearfully at times, the sudden death of his or her partner for a face-saving, guilt-free, or even a heroic ending of a marriage that looks good on the outside but feels suffocating on the inside.

Crises may determine or strengthen actions being considered. I still recall vividly family crises early in my life, and personal decisions that came out of them. During one particularly difficult period I resolved to leave home to escape family conflict and turmoil and to seek a better life. I began leaving home emotionally by the age of twelve, knowing that I would leave physically within a few years. With the conviction that I would leave, I felt freedom to start being different before leaving.

There was rebelliousness in my behavior, but there also was a strong desire and need to get ready to live in a larger world. I found that I could go against some of the family norms and find sanctions beyond the family. Two minor examples will illustrate. Since my father almost drowned as a boy he saw going into the water as dangerous and forbade it. As a small boy I went fishing often, and while at the creeks and ponds stayed to learn to swim. I kept that pleasing secret from my family for at least two years, but friends my age and a few adults knew about it and approved it. Another injunction was against dancing. Members of my family did not dance; it was prohibited, bad. I learned fairly early and made no secret of it. Eventually my immediate family—although not some aunts and uncles —learned to accept the "wayward" behavior that made my life different from theirs.

FANTASY AND HOPE

Throughout many pages of this book anecdotes are presented in which people picture themselves and their experiences in varied situations. These fantasy scenes, sometimes called guided imagery, are not entirely imaginary in the sense of being unreal or escapes from what we feel. They are especially real in that they represent feelings for which we may have no words. Some of the scenes may be like those many of us experience when we seek to explore and discover feelings within ourselves.

Guided fantasies are projections. We project ourselves into scenes or feelings and watch and hear ourselves. We have dialogues in our fantasies. We may reach an impasse. We may get lost in too many words and not know what we feel. At other times, words with which to describe our feelings may not come. Through fantasizing scenes from the past, present, or future, feelings that have been covered up may reappear. The opposite may occur. Feelings that appear may, in fantasy, evoke memories and scenes out of our experiences. Thus our feelings and experiences may get connected through our fantasies.

Through fantasy experiences we may discover our attitudes and conflicts; we may come upon sources of our anxiety. We may relinquish some of our self-control and gain access to feelings that we have put into protective custody somewhere within us because they were too painful. We may get in touch with secret or disowned parts of our emotional life that we have tucked away for reasons unknown.

In fantasy and imagery, important beginnings of change in our lives can be stirred because we are able to imagine ourselves feeling and acting differently. From imagination come the seeds of possibility and hope. Through hope we can feel inner strivings and personal power.

2. Untangling Conflicts Within

If I am to dissolve the crippling anxiety and halt the energy drain brought by conflicts in my life, I need to resolve and learn to tolerate them. Conflicts within and with others often are natural. Learning to deal with them also can become a natural process. Managing them becomes especially difficult, however, when conflict-related emotions and events become veiled and secret. Understanding internal strife becomes difficult also when I fear the consequences of acknowledging beliefs, feelings, and other hidden parts of myself that I do not like. For example, I may believe, almost secretly, that I am fragile and will fall apart—never to come back together again—if I let myself know the dark, angry, censored side that goes with my bright, happy, open side. Yet discovering ways to uncover the hidden facets of myself is a part of conflict resolution and relief.

FEELING STUCK

Conflicts may arise from decisions to be made. When we know what we want, decisions are almost automatic. But there are times when we feel uncertain, unable to make choices. Big decisions which influence our lives and families may come easily or may cause turmoil. They may bring agonizing conflict when our logic and common sense do not match our emotions and intuition. When we act contrary to our logic, we may wonder whether we are acting irresponsibly on impulse. We may wonder whether our emotions hold some secret knowledge that can be trusted. We may know that when we act contrary to our emotions, we are sometimes dissatisfied. Caught in the conflict of our logic and our emotions, we may feel stuck and do nothing at all. A job decision faced by Bob, a young Ph.D. student, illustrates such a dilemma.

Bob's degree was to be awarded in five weeks. He had been offered a teaching and research position in a western university, and he dropped by my office to "share the good news."

"It's the kind of job I have dreamed of getting," he told me. "I am fortunate; it fits my plans, and it comes just at the right time." As Bob talked, his enthusiasm faded. His conflicted feelings became conspicuous as he casually mentioned how long he had delayed his decision. "The letter came a couple of weeks ago, and I must let them know this week."

Words ordinarily used to express enthusiasm, hopefulness, and joy took on tones of confusion, conflict, and hesitation. His words were saying, "I should go," but his feelings were shouting, "No!" Listening, I

29

kept getting the impression that Bob had decided, at some level, not to accept the position. If my impressions were accurate, he could not yet acknowledge this decision to himself. Decisions based only on our feelings are suspect—sometimes rightly so—particularly when we do not know why we feel as we do. Bob had no good reasons to back up a decision not to go; he had only reasons to accept. Still, he could not bring himself to accept. He was stuck.

To explore possible obstacles to making a decision I asked Bob to "assume for now that you have turned down the offer. Think of the person who would be most difficult to tell, and imagine that you are writing a letter explaining your decision." Instantly Bob began his letter aloud: "Dear Dad..." He paused and told how difficult it would be to tell his father who, elderly and ill, had sustained himself with the hope of seeing Bob get a Ph.D. and become a university teacher. Bob felt pulled to accept the post to please his father. He felt an urgency to accept out of fear that this might be the best offer he would get. But what would be required for Bob either to trust his feelings and say no, or to trust his reasoning and say yes? One point was clear: he had no doubts about his enthusiasm for teaching in a college setting.

I was puzzled about what was holding back his decision, and wondered whether or not he was tied to where he lived now, whether he wanted to be nearer his father than the new job would allow, or whether the location was important in some other way. I asked Bob to assume that he had accepted the position and to imagine writing to his father describing the trip to his new job. He made three starts in his letter aloud before he could get himself on his imaginary journey. His car broke down; he got lost; on the third try he was en route. The signs were clear that getting there, even in his imagination, was going to be difficult. Still he did not know why. His frustrations grew.

After two days of restlessness and self-searching, Bob decided to turn down the job without knowing clearly why. His letter declining the offer was surprisingly easy to write. After he made the decision his conflict eased. He was still concerned, however, with whether or not he would get other offers and with where he wanted to go.

A month later Bob received the offer of a similar position in a university in the southeast. Immediate acceptance was natural and free from conflict. Only at this point was Bob fairly certain that the main cause of his conflict was the homelike pull of the southeastern region of the United States. When faced with the prospect of living elsewhere, he had felt empty and indecisive.

After Bob had declined the offer in the west, I mentioned to him that several years ago I tacked a large map of the United States on the wall of my utility room (it was too distracting in my study) and found pleasure in looking at it and imagining where I wanted to travel during different seasons. I would also try to sense my feelings while imagining living in different parts of the country. With increasing frequency and intensity I felt a desire to return to the southwest, a region where I had once lived. For Bob the pull turned out to be the southeast. Fortunately, he had a chance to respond to his pull in that direction.

If we can listen around and beyond the edges to the nuances of what we can say and feel about the pros and cons of a decision we are facing, we might discover that our feelings often are not whimsical. We may find that there is good sense underlying what we do or fail to do. The trying task is to tease out the patterns of those feelings that may lie hidden within and to understand how they are influencing us. This is especially necessary when we have become indecisive and feel unable to come to grips with seemingly incompatible alternatives.

BEYOND THE "HOW CAN I . . ."

I have spent hours listening to individuals who have felt conflicted and have sought advice on "how" to do a particular thing—get along with a spouse, be happy in a job, change a particular behavior—only to discover later that they *did not* want to change. The "how to" questions do cause conflict and often are legitimate concerns. At times, however, they are less relevant than the question: Do I really want to? Listening to conflicts beyond the "how's" may yield information we need to know. We may not have to be so concerned about *how to decide* or *how to change* if we can resolve our conflicts in deciding *that we want to*. Put another way, if we are certain about the *what*, the *how to* may bring less conflict and be less difficult to accomplish.

George, a psychologically sophisticated young resident in psychiatry, concluded a brief description of himself during our first interview, by saying, "All my life I have felt insecure, inadequate really. I'm passive-aggressive, manipulative, and sometimes a little devious." "Do you want to change that pattern of behavior? " I asked. "Not now," he replied. "It serves me well." We immediately moved to conflicts more pressing at the moment.

Andrea, an attractive twenty-one-year-old woman, said in a therapy group that she wanted to learn *how not to be* so dumb. To those of us in the group, Andrea seemed bright and perceptive. Rather than to offer her ready assurances that she was indeed smart, not dumb, we asked her to tell us *what*, in her eyes, made her seem dumb. Immediately she replied, "My boyfriend says I am. There are almost no topics I can discuss deeply and intelligently in social gatherings or at work. I burned out a bearing on my car instead of detecting the symptoms in time to get preventive maintenance." Her case for her dumbness was not especially convincing. Yet she felt caught in conflict between believing she was dumb and wishing she were not.

Members of the group joined Andrea in exploring what benefits she might get out of seeing herself as dumb. With warm support from others present she acknowledged that by acting dumb she avoided many threatening situations. Devastating criticism from her boyfriend was minimized. She need not risk her ideas in discussions of political and social problems. Serious thought about going to graduate school was out of the question. (Andrea's grades and admission test scores were high.) All these and similar situations were threatening demands that could be made upon Andrea if she did not see herself as dumb.

As Andrea's uses of being seen as dumb became clearer to her, she felt a bit sad, but began facing the prospect of losing this part of herself that she had cultivated carefully, and that she both liked and disliked. She also felt relief as her case for dumbness began to crumble. She experienced mixed feelings of excitement and fear when she envisioned herself living in more venturesome ways.

In weeks ahead Andrea discovered that she needed less and less to fall back on her "dumb" self-picture and defensive pattern. She became more able to own and act upon the capabilities she possessed. And Andrea's decision *to want to change* and to risk new behavior was especially important. With that decision her major feelings of conflict subsided. It was important also that we did not get caught up in Andrea's question of *how not to be so dumb* before exploring *what* was dumb about her and *what* she got out of it.

WHAT IS MISSING?

At some periods of my life I have felt caught in a web of routine activities and unchanging relationships, living what I regarded to be a colorless and uninteresting life. My vitality was slipping away, almost imperceptibly. At such times I have felt trapped in conflict between the more acceptable features of my life that "should" satisfy me and the disquieting feelings that my life was not satisfying. I have felt locked into patterns that were fairly comfortable, but monotonously boring. Stanley, a businessman in his early forties, was in a similar predicament when I first met him.

Stanley had hit a slump. He had lost much of his capacity to care about what he was doing and about himself, and had become so embedded in his daily life and surroundings that he could get no promising perspective on his future. He had quit taking risks in his business, had begun to avoid old friends and to shun new relationships. He was on his way to becoming a psychological shut-in.

On face he appeared successful, and actually was in some ways. He liked his family and he liked where he lived; he earned enough money. He liked being rooted, but disliked his deepening rut. He found comfort in the predictability of his daily life, but feared that he was somehow trapped. He was puzzling over whether or not he really was doing what he wanted to do with his life. There was a constant tension in the delicate balance of his conflicts. His inner dialogue would not stop. "I have everything to make me happy, but I'm not happy." "I like being here, but I need a change." "I like my business, but I'm bored." "I have everything I need, but I want something else." "Something is missing." "What is it? What is it?" Stanley continued to talk to himself, but he was unable to listen. He could not find clues to the puzzle of what was missing.

In Stanley's eyes his conflicts seemed too unjustified, too small, even too ridiculous to do anything about, because "there is simply no cause for them." In his eyes, too many other people were much worse off, and this meant that he did not deserve help. He would be self-indulgent, weak, to acknowledge the need, much less deliberately to seek assistance in finding a way out of his dilemma. He was well fortified with excuses to avoid letting someone else in on his problems. He did not want to burden his family more than he had already. He felt uncomfortable revealing too much of himself to friends. And how could he share intimately with a stranger?

Stanley finally became sufficiently depressed and frightened about his situation to seek help, to talk about how his ways of thinking and feeling about his life were out of balance. He had not been exaggerating the desirable features of his life. They did exist. He had been using them, however, to deny his unhappy side. He hoped that if he recited them enough to himself, his unhappiness would go away. He also had been using the positive features to deny the possibility that someone else might be able to help him look at his situation in a different perspective.

When someone else could listen to the depth and pervasiveness of his conflicts, his discontentment, and his depression—without minimizing his feelings of being lost—Stanley could begin to acknowledge more fully that he did, indeed, want more out of life, regardless of what he already had. As he became more able to listen to his deep longings—and not just the reasons why he should feel satisfied—his hopes and optimism slowly emerged again. He began to discover that acknowledging his dissatisfactions and exploring avenues for life changes did not necessarily require drastic reconstruction of his personality, his life style, or his immediate relationships. He could then relinquish the deep fear of the unknown that he had harbored secretly within, a fear that made listening to himself and self-examination a dreadful journey upon which to embark.

As his fear subsided, his ability to express and experience his feelings increased. He became more willing and able to understand connections between the highs and the lows in his life, to see that both were vital parts of himself, and that neither could be disowned, no matter how hard he tried.

Allowing seemingly incongruous facets of himself to exist and then owning them as integral ingredients in his makeup were difficult tasks for him. Yet this was the first step toward change for Stanley. He could effect little change over elements of his life that he continued to deny. Put simplistically, Stanley could not begin to change or to allow change to occur until he claimed the behavior he wanted to change as his own. In seeking to disallow his conflicts and inconsistencies, he increased them. As paradoxical as it may seem, we often need to hear and to own more fully, not less so, the feelings, including the conflicts, that we are trying to change or diminish in importance.

I meet others who are confronted with conflicts like mine and Stanley's—who are content with some features of their lives but who are also discontented. Such people want life to be better and then feel lost and unable to listen to themselves and to tease out what seems to be missing. There are common threads in such dilemmas, but not always common reactions to them. We may gradually slip from boredom to feelings of hopelessness as our vitality ebbs. As we lose vigor we also may feel diminished power to influence our personal lives and activities around us. Lacking influence, we may sink into mild depression and then despair.

The pervasive fear that life is passing us by may lead us to defend against our fear by further withdrawal into apathy. We may deny the fear and try to escape through the use of drugs, alcohol, sexual promiscuity, or flights into different forms of play, work, and new life styles. Or we may drift along without much of an orientation to time, vacillating between feelings of vague, free-floating anxiety and numbed detachment from our lives. Or again, we may become able to give in to our feelings of aimlessness, fear, or despair. And at last we may become willing to risk letting down our guards to feel the pain, to know our hidden feelings, and to face what might be there, hoping eventually to regain sufficient power and self-esteem to rekindle our hopes for a life renewed.

3. Patterns of Conflicts With Others

Conflicts not only wrench us within but lead us to distort ways we see others and let them see us. Examination of tension-producing relationships and incidents in our lives may lead us to deeper understanding of the ingredients of our conflicts.

DISCOVERING THE PATTERNS

Recently I conducted a workshop for twelve people who were searching for better ways to understand and handle conflicts. They hoped to sharpen their ability to see their own styles of entering, maintaining, and breaking off relationships. To achieve their purposes, members joined me in looking back and studying our behavior—our repertoires, so to speak, for relating to other people.

Imagine yourself as a participant in a group with these purposes. There are eleven others. You may know some of them casually from earlier introductions, but most are strangers. You are sitting in a comfortable room. You want to be natural, but you do not feel natural. You have so many feelings that you cannot sort them out. You are a bundle of conflicts. Suddenly you wonder: What are other people here feeling? Will they share their honest reactions? How might they react to you if you express what you really believe and feel—assuming you know what you really believe and feel?

As you picture yourself in the group, try to sense the conflicts you might feel and the ways you identify with the behavior of other members. Early in the experience, participants began to get glimpses of how they acted and how others in turn reacted to them. Two people, for example, felt torn between shyness and aggressiveness. They showed their aggressive side when they voiced provocative, dogmatic statements of opinion. Later one of them acknowledged, "I was frightened and wanted to cover it up by acting like I knew a great deal." The other explained, "I am naturally shy, fearful of being left out. I intended for my comments to break the ice." A third member who felt knowledgeable about how to act in such a group, yet fearful of being in this one, made an immediate bid for influence by insisting that people talk only about "what you *feel*, not what you *think*." These group members, feeling different conflicts within, set themselves up as targets and drew fire, negative reactions. Their aggression was met with aggression that heightened their feelings of conflict.

Some participants felt uneasy about conflict situations and tried constantly to smooth them over. When one young man's overly protective behavior was mirrored back to him, he withdrew from the group in the manner of a helpless, hurt, little boy sulking in the corner. Withdrawing from others was a tendency of his, he discovered, when he felt hurt and treated unfairly. Another member, Eve, was liked at first for her politeness and consideration for others. Later, members felt frustrated and confronted her with her evasive maneuvers that kept them from getting to know her better. Eve's constant smile and friendly, inviting eyes that darted around the room from person to person offered promises of friendship that Eve never kept. She was protecting herself from others through politeness and promises of more to come. The desire to have close friends and the risk of opening herself up for friendship left Eve conflicted.

There were other ways of covering up feelings of conflict during the workshop, just as there are in other settings. Common among them were the uses of jokes and humor to cover up feelings of fear, anger, or affection. Intellectualizations, that is, discussing personal matters in an objective, detached manner as though they were impersonal, also were used to hide a variety of feelings tinged with conflict.

Another thing soon became apparent. We often pay too big a price to be liked. As a consequence, we feel conflicted. Our need to be liked, even by people we dislike, may cause us to lose our genuineness. We may be patronizing, awkward, self-conscious, and act in other inappropriate ways as a result of excessive self-monitoring in our efforts to make a good impression. Such unnatural behavior may leave us feeling dissatisfied.

We may live in fear that a catastrophe will result if we are disliked. People in our workshop found out that if someone did not like them, expectations of catastrophe usually did not materialize. Even feelings of hurt and rejection were not so hard to experience as expected. In most instances the ability to participate in open discussions of likes and dislikes reduced attendant feelings of conflict. Individuals who learned to acknowledge feelings of dislike and to accept being disliked discovered that they became more able to develop closer, more authentic, even more loving relationships. Similarly, individuals who could accept the differences in how they felt about one another found that their differences, not just their similarities, could become bridges to solid relationships.

When in conflict, behavior is more distorted and restricted. As workshop participants saw examples of such patterns of behavior, they became more able to tolerate inconsistent and conflicted behavior. There was an upward spiraling effect. As they became more tolerant of themselves and one another in conflict situations, they also became more able, often eager, to reveal previously guarded feelings. As the level of sharing increased and deepened, the feelings of conflict decreased.

Most of the people in the workshop discovered that, despite years of practice, their efforts to hide their conflicted feelings often were unsuccessful. Facial expressions, gestures, voice, words, and general manner revealed more than the individual had suspected. More often than not, relief rather than disappointment was experienced when their cover-up behavior became known. Occasionally, however, some members were sufficiently skillful and well-practiced to keep their conflicts hidden. But there was a price for them to pay. Those who were covered up to others often became covered up to themselves as well.

WARFARE AT WORK

Among people with whom we work, conflict may be inevitable. When cleavages mount and relationships

41

begin to rupture, an outsider who can listen and hear each person and conflicted factions sometimes can increase the quality of their listening and understanding. Last year I was invited by a superintendent of schools to meet with faculty members, counselors, assistant principal, and the principal—thirty-four in all—from a junior high school in a large city school system. Twenty-eight faculty members had signed a petition to get the principal fired. The superintendent and his staff had decided that intensive efforts to work out the conflicts would be more desirable than to fire the principal or the teachers. Some of the teachers and administrators in the school system who had participated in human relations and communications workshops I had conducted during the two previous years suggested that a communications workshop in a retreat setting away from the city might help.

I agreed to conduct this workshop feeling both exhilaration and apprehension as I wondered whether it would be a significant breakthrough in relationships, a damaging failure, or simply a neutral venture that would have no impact. Would I get caught up in the arguments and issues, unwittingly take one side or the other, or get trapped by some of my own inner conflicts during the experience? Would I be able to hear all the views and feelings expressed? Could I represent them fairly? I clearly wanted to make a difference. But if my needs were too great I could become a part of the problem and botch the entire proceedings.

The fact that the workshop was on a weekend and participants were traveling some seventy miles from home could precipitate negative reactions. School people, like many others, want their weekends free. Moreover, any fear and threat they felt in being strongly nudged by the superintendent to confront the situation could be expressed in anger and aggression, could be covered up with a veneer of social amenities, or could be expressed in some unexpected way.

During Friday night and Saturday morning sessions we worked sometimes in small groups and other times as one large group on communication problems. We used listening and sharing exercises to identify biases and patterns of letting others know what we thought and felt about both safe and controversial topics. School policies and decision-making processes were used as discussion topics through which we attempted to get at conflict situations and to examine the processes and patterns of communication.

By Saturday afternoon I began to feel that we were going through the motions of identifying problems of conflict, but that nothing significant was happening. We were on the surface; the level of trust was not high; opinions and attitudes were not being expressed openly. Finally I shared these impressions and asked for reactions from others. Some of the participants pictured the situation much the way I did. Others said that they thought everyone was being genuine and open. Still others thought that the workshop could be only a charade at best, since no one there would ever feel free to say what he or she thought.

I pulled my chair to the middle of the room and invited those who wanted to work on the conflicts within the school and among persons present to join me. Our task would be to try to express what we thought and felt and to try equally hard to hear persons whose attitudes and views might be quite different. The principal and seven teachers moved quickly to the middle of the room. I said that I would do what I could to help to get a full and complete picture of the views they expressed, to sharpen their differences as well as to recognize their similarities and agreements, and then look with them at the consequences of what they were doing there. Someone immediately suggested that I needed to be "the referee." I have done various kinds of refereeing and recognized that this might be a part of the task, along with coaching, teaching, and especially listening in order to play back what was happening.

In a few minutes accusations, defenses, attacks, and counterattacks came, hot and furious. More teachers moved into the verbal fray. The principal had supporters to whom he listened for guidance. Other teachers accused him of being an autocrat, a dictator who set rules by edict, who conducted faculty meetings without listening to them, and who was more interested in keeping the school orderly than in helping children learn. The principal and those who supported him accused some teachers of being irresponsible, lax in discipline, disloyal, unwilling to have their work evaluated. He also accused them of trying to make him an outsider since he was newer in the school than most of them. Both sides had valid points to make in a literal sense, but their antagonisms toward each other led them to state their views and to express their feelings in extremes.

Regularly I stopped the heated discussions—blew the whistle like a referee—and played back what I thought was being expressed. I checked out who was hearing what, and asked for participants to identify exaggerated positions and to restate their positions more accurately if they could. Persons were gradually becoming more open and expressive as they talked to one another. An obvious exaggeration occasionally led to outbursts of laughter which released some of the tension. But the climate remained predominantly serious and tense. Some areas of differences and of agreement were identified and openly acknowledged. Gradually the accusations became fewer and were leveled with less anger. As the criticisms decreased so did the tension. Administrators and faculty members little by little began to run out of grievances and to hear each other more clearly. As they became more able to listen, they began to discover that they could influence one another, and could influence the principal. With increased influence, their self-esteem and respect for one another seemed to mount.

The Sunday session ran late into the afternoon. By the end of the workshop, the faculty and the principal had discovered some productive ways to talk and to listen to one another. They were emotionally spent and physically exhausted. Yet they were exhilarated and relieved in the knowledge that they had turned anger and conflict into attitudes of cooperation and a desire to deepen trust. No one pretended that this era of good feeling would last, but there was hope that they could work together for awhile.

I left the workshop wondering what would happen next. My worst fantasy was that a new petition would be circulated on Monday; my best hope was that the staff members would continue to talk and to listen to one another.

Eleven months later I received a follow-up report by phone from the superintendent's office. The junior high school, I learned, had been evaluated recently and had come out with high ratings. The principal and teachers had attributed the favorable report to their communications workshop and to their continued hard work in improving their working relationships. But the follow-up report I received was not the reason for the phone call. The main purpose was to inquire about holding another workshop. It seemed that the teachers of another school within the district, an elementary school this time, had petitioned to fire *their* principal.

4. Couples in Conflict

When conflict with someone with whom we live is constantly denied or suppressed, the relationship suffers. And when the conflict continues to be evaded, our irritations and frustrations may pop out in ways and places that baffle and frighten us, especially if we do not know the incidents and causes to which these frustrations are connected. We forget that anger may be the other side of love, that intimacy may be born of conflict, and that deep intimacy is unlikely to survive without healthy and openly expressed conflict. Conflict long harbored without resolution or management may erupt like a smoldering volcano and wreak irreparable devastation on a relationship. When conflict is accompanied by guilt for being bad, weak, or unfair, we lose self-esteem. Anecdotes describing conflicts between couples illustrate some of these patterns and their consequences.

NO CONFLICT, NO LOVE

A couple may be free from conflict because they have learned to confront and work out conflict situations regularly. Or their freedom from such tensions may mean that they no longer care. They may have slipped into routines smoothed by indifference, even apathy. Douglas and Jennie seem to have no conflicts. They have been married six years. Doug is a moderately successful insurance man. He sees people all day and comes home to relax, putter in his shop, have a drink, and watch television. Jennie is a nurse who is on her feet all day and comes home tired. She fixes dinner while Doug putters. They take occasional weekend trips together to see friends, to take in a professional football game, or just to get out of town. They like one another, find living together easy, sometimes enjoyable.

Jennie usually knows what Doug thinks and feels about most subjects that come up before he speaks. Jennie is just as predictable to Doug. They seldom raise their voices to one another. There is nothing to fuss about. Neither wants children. Both like their jobs reasonably well. They have good health.

Why would they come for counseling? They recently spent a week apart. Surprisingly, each enjoyed the other's absence. More surprisingly, they talked about it and began to wonder what it meant about their lives together. Had they shut themselves down to one another? Were they drying up emotionally? They became aware that they were lonely in their routines. During their marriage they had subdued their minor irritations with one another. They had also dampened sparks of excitement and any creative power they might have to find a more interesting life with one another. They had ruled out conflict with one another, and with it had ruled out their ability to have intimate contact.

How might listening to them help? After an initial interview with the two of them, I saw them separately for a few sessions. As they began to feel heard in their boredom and loneliness, urges for something more began to stir. Then came spurts of desire to experiment with uncovering and exploring a host of feelings. Following separate interviews, they were seen together, and they literally practiced talking and listening to one another about day-to-day events, minor irritations, and small pleasures.

As they awakened to themselves and to one another, they began to touch on areas of conflict. Jennie felt shut out and irritated because Doug spent every Saturday morning puttering around the shop or visiting with a friend when she wanted him to do errands and go shopping with her. He did not know that. Doug complained that Jennie spent endless hours talking on the phone to friends and to her mother, leaving him alone. Moreover, he had been angry with her mother for two years and had buried the feeling, even though they all lived in the same city. Jennie knew neither of these feelings. And so it went.

At first, they were astonished at the irritations, big and small, that surfaced. Then as they expressed and listened to their conflicts, they began to rediscover interest in one another and new feelings of intimacy. They began to learn and relearn the give-and-take, the yielding, the open and honest bartering that takes place when people care about one another, want things from one another, and seek cooperation. But first they had to get beyond the indifference and complacency that had crept into their lives, almost unnoticed.

EVADING CONFLICTS

Some couples evade conflicts out of fear of consequences. Jim and Terri, in their early twenties, have been married three years. During their first counseling session she says that she is losing interest in him and does not want to respond to him with love or affection. She sees Jim as compliant, passive, and overeager to please. Sometimes, however, he is stubborn and unresponsive to her. Jim agrees, and adds that he wants to change, to be more assertive and less dependent.

If you listen to Terri carefully, you can hear a talking-down tone in her voice when she talks to Jim. She sounds like a sometimes stern, sometimes solicitous mother. If you listen to her talking to the counselor, her voice sounds more like that of a little girl talking to a father. You make a note to play these tones back to check out what feelings go with them. But not yet. She and Jim are too much concerned at the moment with her lack of responsiveness to him and with his decreasing self-esteem.

During the second session Jim begins to react to Terri's criticism, but his manner is like that of a boy talking back to a mother. The tightness of Jim's mouth, the tenseness in his erect sitting posture, and the heightened pitch in his voice suggest irritation. You ask him if he feels frustration or anger and he quickly replies that "expressing anger is wrong." He has grown up in a family in which no one should be angry; no one should express it—ever! Jim's anger is buried.

When a couple comes to talk about their conflicts, if you listen carefully, you can hear the intent underlying what they say and do. Is the intent of one to blame or to win a dominant position? Is the intent of the other to submit, to lose the fight and win martyrdom? In win-lose situations both lose because the basis for mutuality, openness, and love is eroded.

While listening to Terri and Jim, your over-all impression might be of an element of competitiveness that has not yet reached a win-lose or an overkill level. For the most part you hear softness and concern, expressions that sound like desires to improve the relationship. Both seem eager to work. They do need help in listening to themselves and one another, in teasing out and expressing their feelings, and in searching out the patterns of their conflicts.

Some of the patterns in Terri and Jim's relationship begin to appear. Terri is attracted to men who are dominant and strong, and at the same time she is afraid of them. She feels excitement in discovering whether or not she can measure up to them. But she risks losing a part of herself if they should want to take her over. Occasionally, however, it is nice, she feels, to be taken over and "cared for by a strong male." Terri wants Jim to be more independent of her and more assertive in their relationship. Because he is passive she does not feel responsive or attracted to him. The rub: While she wants Jim to show strength and dominance, she treats him like a dependent little boy. With him she feels safe, but unexcited. Dare she risk his growing up in the relationship? Terri says, "Yes," but her behavior at this point sounds more like, "No."

Jim wants to please Terri; he is afraid to be assertive for fear he will lose her. Still, in his cautiousness and desire to please, he is losing his appeal to her and his own self-esteem. He does not want to be controlled by her, yet it is nice to feel that she is a strong, self-reliant woman "who does not need too much from me." Should he risk losing her, or having to work out a new relationship with her? Having a history of holding back and of feeling guilty over the slightest criticism makes change more difficult. Jim says, "Yes, I want to change and not allow you to control me so much," but his behavior sounds more like, "I can't."

Jim and Terri have begun to feel the conflicts. They are beginning to see the interlocking twists and turns in their relationship. They are getting their feelings to the surface and relating them to specific incidents.

Seeing their patterns of conflict is not enough for Terri and Jim. Having seen them, they begin to retreat in fear, like groundhogs afraid of their shadows. Their relationship has been based largely on the need for safety and a childish dependence upon one another. If they risk letting go of one another to discover their own separate strengths and autonomy, they risk also the discovery that they may not love one another with sufficient depth and compatibility for their relationship to endure. Too, they risk facing the question of whether or not they are capable of making durable and loving commitments to anyone.

Having peeked at changes needed for their relationship to become more satisfying and having sensed the possible loss of the security they have achieved, they hold back and cling to one another even more than before. They hope for a miracle to change them so that Terri will somehow feel passion for Jim and Jim will get love and affection from Terri. Meanwhile each becomes ripe for other relationships to fill their unmet needs. Instead of a miracle, a third person or some other undeniable incident may intrude and disrupt their relationship. A crisis that intensifies the conflict, not a miracle, may propel them beyond the barrier of fear that locks them into a mildly conflicted, unsatisfactory, but known and relatively safe relationship.

BEYOND HOPE

The irritations, disagreements, and tension-producing situations arising out of deep conflict may become escalated and lead to destructive behavior toward ourselves and those around us. The consequences of

51

devastating overkill kinds of conflict in war, politics, and a vast array of human enterprises, including marriage, are well known to most of us.

You listen to another couple. Curt and Harriet are in their late thirties, have been married sixteen years, and have two children, twelve and fourteen. They need to figure out what to do about their marriage and living arrangements. First you talk with them separately. Curt sees Harriet as a middle-aged woman who is trying to recapture her youth by chasing a new life style with younger men. Harriet sees herself as a lonely woman, exploited in marriage, youthful in spirit, and seeking freedom from the shackles of a conventional marriage. She sees Curt as a stodgy, rigid man who has Victorian attitudes toward sex, and who takes too little responsibility for household chores and for disciplining the children. In her eyes, he depends on her for maid services, even though she works full time outside. Curt sees himself as a man of reason, willing to recognize his shortcomings, to participate in managing the house and the children. He makes clear, however, that he has no desire to be overly meticulous in supervising the children or cleaning the house.

Next you talk with Harriet and Curt together. They announce a decision to divorce. Lack of money prevents them from separating immediately. They need to reach an accommodation to coexist in the same house for a few months until separation is financially feasible and disruption for the children is minimized. You soon discover that feelings of conflict and resentment borne so long now get triggered by what appear to be relatively unimportant incidents. Harriet accuses Curt of neglecting to clean up the house, especially the dog hair on the living room sofa, when it is his turn. Curt lashes back that she is the last one to leave the house and fails to put the dog out of the house into the backyard. He adds additional charges. The battle is underway. At one level they are in conflict over household chores; at another they are fighting over who is to blame for their present plight; at still another they are in conflict over the loss of influence with one another. Each feels powerless, hopeless, and diminished in self-esteem. They no longer are listening to one another, and lack any further desire to try. Both want out of the relationship, out of the house; both feel locked in.

If you had hopes that you as an interested person would listen and seek harmony and understanding, your hopes are soon dashed. This fight has been going on for a long time. Harriet and Curt are desperate. Their energy is being drained in a struggle to survive. Their attitudes toward one another have taken on a lethal quality. Each tries to transfer blame to the other, but is haunted by the occasional awareness that he or she has failed, is also to blame, should be able to change things, should be able to get free from all this, if only— Only what?

Your efforts to listen sensitively and your desire to arbitrate fairly are brought to bear to make the struggle easier, to make separation less destructive, to work out a temporary truce. You end up facing indisputable evidence that the relationship is beyond hope, that with the freedom to choose lovers and spouses goes the freedom to unchoose them. And such a decision is painful to carry out. Your help is limited. You may begin to feel a sense of helplessness, perhaps despair. You find that you need to learn over and over again that you can care about these people, you can hurt with them, but they are not in your hands. You only can be at hand if they need and want you to be.

After couples part, embittered, reduced if not shattered in self-esteem, they have work to do in understanding what happened to them. They can do this work separately or together. The latter is often difficult—usually impossible. This is true for Harriet and Curt. They are too caught up in survival to look back thoughtfully and learn new ways of being in relationships with someone else. Understanding what happened is important, however, to avoid the same traps in future relationships. Untangling the web of conflict and unhappiness is essential for them if they are to gain freedom to try new relationships without the pessimism that they, too, will fail.

UNDERSTANDING WHAT HAPPENED

Rita and Steve had been divorced a year and a half. Rita moved to another city and sought counseling to adjust to a new life situation and to learn more about the conflicts that disrupted her marriage. She still cared deeply about Steve but acknowledged that the relationship had become intolerable for both of them. During the months of counseling she explored a myriad of problems in her marriage. She was angry at Steve's parents for treating him like a little boy and for keeping him from being a "more grown-up husband." She was dependent on Steve for money. She felt no freedom to go shopping for herself or to spend money for social and recreational activities without his permission. She resented asking, and seldom did.

Steve did not talk to her about his daily activities in business. She was not sure whether he was shielding her or withholding information, but she felt shut out. She resented having to push him to make big decisions —to build the new house they could well afford—and lesser decisions—to join *this* club and *that* social group. After decisions were made, he seemed to enjoy the results. She felt pleased but also angry for having to needle and wheedle so much.

Positive facets of the marriage were discussed. Steve was an excellent father—thoughtful, loving, eager to spend time with the children in many ways. Rita was irked occasionally that he was the good guy while she was the disciplinarian. But she found out that she could be a good guy too, if she wanted to, and that he would take responsibility for setting limits for the children.

Through the months she worked on her earlier conflicts with Steve, on relationships in her present job, and on returning to graduate school. She learned to express her anger more freely toward herself, toward Steve, toward his parents. She could sort out where her anger belonged and where it was misplaced, that is, aimed at the wrong target. She began to discover that on too many occasions she had not made her desires and feelings known to Steve, and that in still other situations she overreacted and pushed harder than necessary to get herself heard. While she was not vindictive or inclined to put the full blame on Steve, she could more clearly see his part, as well as her own, in the breakup of the marriage. During the period of separation and divorce, Rita was also discovering more independence. She did not need to ask permission about how to spend money or manage an increasing number of responsibilities in her life.

Steve started visiting the children on weekends every two or three weeks. During his visits she told him about her counseling experiences—what she was working on, what she was feeling and thinking about him, about herself, about his parents, and about what happened to the marriage. He had been working in his own way to sort out his views of what happened to them. Long hours were spent talking about their lives together and apart, not so much with the idea of placing blame or patching up the relationship as understanding the ingredients that led to conflicts and blow-ups. They found that they still liked one another and could enjoy being together.

Rita continued in the counseling sessions, and Steve asked if he might join her as often as he could when he came to the city to visit. During their interviews together they reviewed numerous incidents out of the past and compared ways each looked at them, then and now. Steve was surprised that Rita had felt like a little girl who was coming resentfully to her father to ask for money. They were in different circumstances now; Rita had funds of her own and could look at this problem more freely. Steve did not know that Rita had cared about what his days had been like at the office. She had never asked. Strange, they thought, how they had lived together for so many years and made so many wrong guesses about what each wanted. Rita could air her feelings of resentment about how Steve's parents treated him. But he had seen her as more "mothering" than his own mother, except in handling money. Both were aware of her pressing him for the decisions about building the house and sheltering him at home from her problems with the children.

Steve had resented Rita's unwillingness to play, her seeming lack of interest in going out of town with him and making vacations out of some of his business trips, and her regarding dancing as frivolous. Since the divorce she had come to enjoy dancing and occasional parties, and being a "little frivolous" herself. In talking with Steve about it, she made the unexpected discovery that she had never regarded dancing and adult playing as "proper" for him as her husband. Why would she enjoy other men in play situations and yet see such play as wrong for Steve? She came upon the long-forgotten attitude that she had held toward her own father, whom she saw as irresponsible, neglectful of his wife and children, and who had foolishly put his own hedonistic life style ahead of his family. She had harbored the fear, not based on fact, that Steve would be like her father.

During this period of looking back, Rita and Steve did not talk much about the future. Facing the prospects of getting back together threatened progress both were making in personal growth while separate. They feared falling back into old habits and conflicts. So they entered a dating period with energy placed on what they would do during the weekends he came to town.

In and between counseling sessions, they were learning to listen to one another and to ask for what they wanted and needed. They pinpointed some places where they had failed and found ways to resolve new conflicts that arose. A recent incident illustrates the kind of predicament that had occurred frequently during their marriage. Steve was coming to see Rita and the children for a weekend during his birthday. She asked him what he would like to do. He said in an offhand manner that he would like to have a party with some of the people they had known for years who now lived in the city and with some new people she had met. Rita agreed. After Steve left town she was in a stew.

She had final examinations and had no time to have a dinner party, get out invitations, prepare the food, and get the house ready. She became resentful. Steve was expecting too much of her under these conditions. She was encouraged to phone Steve, to tell him how much pressure she felt, and to suggest alternatives that might be less burdensome. She held back. She was afraid that he would misunderstand or be disappointed. Finally she phoned him, and found out that she had misunderstood. He had expected to take her out for dinner and then after dinner to have a few people drop by. He had not expected an elaborate seated dinner for twelve, but he had not been clear about what he did expect. This incident triggered recollection of numerous other incidents where they had failed to make themselves clear to one another and where the resentments had grown out of proportion.

Weeks later, during their last counseling session, Rita and Steve both were excited. An hour earlier they had gotten a license to be married. They have been remarried almost two years now, and live in a different city. The relationship seems solid, but not without problems. They continue to work in varied ways to keep their relationship alive and healthy. They are trying not to evade their conflicts out of fear, for the consequences of evasion, they have learned, are worse than the fear. They know that not all conflict situations can be dealt with when they occur. They are likely, for example, to back off temporarily from extreme emotional reactions to one another, and come back later to work out their feelings. Conflicts are sometimes escalated and impossible to understand or resolve when emotions are rampant, unless a third person is invited to intervene.

Steve and Rita are learning to make fewer predictions about what the other expects, wants, or believes and to make more inquiries to find out directly. They found out through painful experiences that their predictions often are wrong and rob one another of opportunities to express themselves freely. Too, in checking with one another they find increased spontaneity in how they act. As a consequence, they seem more interesting to one another. To come upon and apply these fairly simple beliefs, Rita and Steve looked back to understand what happened in their relationship, how they triggered and handled their conflicts, and how they could get free from the grip of old ways of behaving that did not serve them well.

After we have weathered the stress of feeling torn with conflict, we may discover a new energy flow and feelings of serenity. After we have teased out and read the signs that tell us the meaning of our conflicts, we may experience heightened self-esteem and increased emotional power to survive. Experiencing ourselves whole after feeling split, and tranquil after feeling turbulent often brings us great hope. We also realize that the need to confront our inconsistencies and conflicts and the self-knowledge that is sometimes held secret within us is not a one-time thing.

5. Catching Your Anger

Anger, fear, and psychological hurt are dominant emotions in conflict situations. These emotions get so intertwined that they are difficult to sort out. We may feel fear, but express anger. A physician friend of mine could not understand why many of his patients were resentful or openly angry with him. He had done nothing to provoke anger. He later understood when he discovered they were fearful he might discover a serious malady and were covering up their fright with anger.

Anger, both that which flares and that which burns slowly, may be an overlay for hurt. A young graduate student became angry when his girlfriend showed interest in other men. Beneath his anger were feelings of hurt and rejection. He wondered if he measured up, if he were worthy of her. He could express self-righteous anger for any slight "wrong" she may have done him, but seldom would he express his self-doubts, jealousy, and hurt.

On the other hand, we may feel anger, but express fear. A young woman in a therapy group showed signs of her fear. Her face was pale and her breathing was shallow; she perspired, and her hands trembled. Upon acknowledging her fright she became aware of the rage ignited within her by a young man in the group who reminded her of her husband who recently had left her. Once she expressed the fear covering her anger, she could let out the anger more openly.

We may need to listen with sensitivity to ourselves and to have others hear us to find out what we do feel. Knowing what we feel is necessary, not so much to express the feeling as to have a clear choice in whether or not to do so. Learning how to rid ourselves of the anger that renews itself almost regularly is a necessary step toward its dissolution. It is also necessary in reaching other feelings, and in vacating the space occupied by the anger to make room for feelings that serve us better.

FACING ANGER

Most of us can recall incidents in which we could sense and face another person's anger, knowing that we were not endangered, that the anger would pass, that it would be resolved somehow. In other instances, however, we did not want to work toward resolution. We, too, were angry and wanted to withdraw or retaliate. We may have sought an advantage and may have needed to win. In an angry win-lose encounter between two persons one may feel humiliated as the loser and the other dominant as the winner. The winner, however, may feel guilt on the one hand or a temporary balm for a weak self-concept on the other. The loser may feel martyrdom or self-righteousness or both. Or he might feel an unhealthy satisfaction in submitting and in having feelings of weakness sustained.

Confronted with the anger of others, we may depersonalize them by writing them off with labels. We may label them, for instance, as "irresponsible, rebellious teenagers," "stodgy, narrow-minded parents," or as something else that categorizes them in ways that preclude our having to deal with them more personally.

As a parent and as one who works with people in therapy, I may regard anger toward me as impersonal, as a reaction against me as an "authority figure," as a person who is a "stand-in" for someone else toward whom the anger is felt. In such instances I am depersonalizing myself, which is sometimes helpful. For if the anger is not directed toward me personally, if it is not an outgrowth of my behavior, looking at it impersonally gives me a perspective from which to work more effectively, free from the other person's anger. At times, however, I need to recognize that the anger is indeed directed toward me. Then it is my task to discover what I am doing to provoke the anger and to listen in more personal terms.

We may err rather consistently, either in taking another person's anger toward us as a personal affront or attack, or in regarding it as impersonal, as having little or nothing to do with us. Frequently I need to reexamine my attitudes in facing anger. I may be overly inclined to deny someone else's anger by seeing it as their problem, when it also is mine.

We may be able to let the anger and aggression of others have impact upon us without the need or desire to retaliate. The question is: How much threat does another person's anger pose to our self-esteem, identity, and freedom? If you have power over me, your anger will be threatening. If I need for you to like me, I will be bothered. If your anger toward me is related to behavior of mine which makes me angry with myself, I may feel vulnerable and defensive. Still, I might be able to acknowledge your anger toward me, along with my own. I am less likely to be bothered by someone else's anger if it is directed toward behavior and actions of mine with which I feel satisfied.

Whether or not we remain intact or become defensive when facing anger will vary according to the situation, the persons involved, and the ways we look at anger and at ourselves when confronted with it. Ideally, I suppose, what we have to present to another person when anger is leveled at us is our sense of self and the desire to be our own persons, separate, but still in relationship.

EXPRESSING ANGER

My ability and willingness to let my anger out is influenced by how I know others and want them to know me. Is expressing anger toward a stranger easier than expressing it toward someone you know? Or is it easier if you know the person? If a stranger fails to stop at a stop sign and drives across the street in front of you, barely missing your car, are you likely to blast your horn or shout in anger? If you react in anger and then notice that it is a friend, how will you feel?

To react angrily to a stranger may be easier. Strangers can be depersonalized, that is, regarded as less human, because we know or pretend to know nothing about them personally. Moreover, we can feel relatively safe and have little need later to preserve our image as "kind, considerate, and reasonable."

On a day-to-day basis we may be more likely to

express anger to our friends, family, and work associates. We may have their permission. They may be safer targets. As a consequence, we may exploit them and abuse our relationship. Still, they are the people from whom we may need and get the most help in managing our anger and in looking back to understand it. If I have a bad day and unleash frustration and anger on my wife and children, will I be able to tell them what led up to my outburst? Working with anger often is a two-way street. They may need to help by encouraging me to talk about it, and by letting me know how it affects them, especially if they can do so before reaching an explosive point. They may need to help me sort out other feelings mixed in with my anger. Sometimes, for example, I cover up fear with anger. For me to discover the fear may enable me to deal with both the fear and the anger.

An incident may illustrate. One of my teenage daughters is over an hour past the time at night she agreed to be home. My first reaction is concern for her safety. She may have had car trouble, an accident, or have been hurt in some way. I feel fear. I attempt to minimize my worry with the thought that she probably forgot the hour and is enjoying being with friends. The thought that she is having a good time while I am worrying about her irritates me. Now I am angry. How could she be so inconsiderate, so irresponsible? Still, I am not sure why she is so late. If I find out that she has been hurt and was unable to let me know, my concern and understanding will grow. But if she hits the door happy and oblivious to the hour, or even if she is apologetic for being late, my anger may surge.

If I can know that my deepest feelings have been fear and concern for her safety, and that my irritation and anger stem from feeling inconvenienced or that they have been used to cover up my fear, I can respond

to her arrival and the total situation more appropriate-
ly. My daughter may need to listen to me, hear me out,
in order for me to get in touch with these layers of
feelings and to become more able to listen to myself
and then to her. We both need to sense the importance
of sorting out our feelings in such situations and not
write one another off in anger as inconsiderate, or with
some other categorical label that bars understanding.

Learning to talk with others about feeling frustrated
and angry with events of the day or with my own
dissatisfactions may be more useful than making
others the target of my feelings. Even if they are a part
of the cause, expressing *that I am angry* or irritated may
be more appropriate than blowing up at them. I
usually feel better for *sharing that I feel angry* than for
verbally *attacking* another person. Moreover, letting
someone know how I feel, rather than firing a salvo of
anger, is another avenue for getting to the feelings
underneath. This less frontal expression causes me less
anxiety and less guilt than blowing up. *Talking about it*
also may enable others to help me get my anger in perspective and reduce the ways it distorts my behavior.

ANGER FELT, NOT SEEN OR HEARD

Have you been around people who give you the
feeling that they are angry, but who do not show you
the signs of anger? They may be pleasant, smiling,
even ingratiating. Their words, if taken literally, may
be kind, but the tone and body language lead you to
feel they must be angry. As you listen you are unable
to validate their anger, but you feel certain that something is awry.

"I never saw my parents angry with one another,"
Leona said in a counseling session. "My mother was a
saint. She really was. She never lost her temper—was

always kind." Leona paused, and then added in a tone with a touch of puzzlement, "An amazing woman."

"Almost unbelievable?" I asked tentatively.

"I've never seen anyone like her. I'm certainly not like her." She spoke as though she had not heard me. She then glanced up and answered abruptly, "Yes, unbelievable." She paused. "But why should I say that? She never gave me reason to doubt her. And another thing! Why should I feel irritated with her?"

There was no way for me to know what Leona's mother was like. I was finding out, however, that Leona believed that she could not measure up to her mother's "goodness" and that she was feeling both guilt and anger for that—anger toward her mother and toward herself.

As parents, some of us may try to hide our anger from our children, sometimes properly so when the anger inappropriately burdens them. But we also may underestimate their sensitivity and their capacity for handling it. If they do sense that we are angry but cannot see or know firsthand what we feel, they are unable to validate their own ways of experiencing our anger. They are deprived of opportunities to learn that anger need not mean rejection and loss of love. They miss opportunities to learn that they may feel and show anger and not be seen as "bad," "sinful," or "unlovable."

While some of us have a distorted picture of the good parent or the good person as free from anger, others have grown up in a sea of anger and turbulent emotions. We may have had enough anger to last us a lifetime and want to back away from it, not experience it or have to deal with it in any form.

Any sign of anger, either verbal or physical, was frightening to Rachel, who was twenty-eight. Even friendly physical contact, such as wrestling, prompted her to withdraw to the corner of the room where she curled up to protect herself. She was afraid. Anger meant violence. She had witnessed its destructiveness as a child. Now she was having trouble relearning ways to allow herself and others to express it. Her energy was spent avoiding it.

We may have trouble getting a perspective on anger and its expression if we do not experience it with people who also can show us love. We also may have trouble getting it in perspective if we are around people who show us only anger and no love.

ANGER SEEN AND HEARD, NOT FELT

Just as we may have felt anger in others despite their failure to verbalize it, we also may have heard the words and seen the motions of anger but not felt the anger. I recall an incident that illustrates how expressions of anger may not convey the anger itself. A few years ago I was invited to conduct a training workshop for mental health workers who worked with groups. Early in the first session four of the dozen participants were hurling epithets, holding pillows for one another to hit with their fists, and were apparently exploding with anger. I watched for several minutes wondering what this exhibition of anger meant. I did not know that these four persons had been in several groups together. However, I soon inferred that they knew each other rather well, since their actions seemed synchronized, almost rehearsed.

As I watched I could not feel their anger. I wondered if I were becoming insensitive, overly fatigued, or afraid and thus denying the realities of such an angry scene. To check out the discrepancy between what looked like anger and my inability to sense it, I asked the participants—two men and two women—if they would stop for a moment. They did. I then asked them if they would be willing to tell us what they were doing.

What we had seen was two women in an argument. One had gotten lost on her way to the workshop and had blamed the other for giving bad directions. This led to the verbal fray. One of the two men involved sided with the woman who gave the directions. The other man had invited himself to join the action by pounding a pillow. We could see clearly that they were exchanging verbal insults and pounding pillows. Still, their behavior seemed lacking in spontaneity and impact. They were not listening to one another.

One person's reply to my inquiry was, "We're blowing off our anger." The others quickly agreed. I asked why they were doing that. One replied: "We have to blow off our anger to get to our other feelings." This seemed reasonable enough. The next question then was, "What feelings do you suppose are underneath your anger?" Again the group of four accepted the response of one who said, "We don't know, but we need to blow off our anger to find out."

Later in the workshop what all of us learned, and what some of us suspected earlier, was that these participants, although perhaps well-intentioned, were not blowing off their anger to discover what was under it. They were going through the rituals of expressing anger to avoid what else might be there. As later events unfolded, we began to experience their deeper feelings of fear and hurt under the ritualistic displays of anger. But first we had to get beyond the defensive wall that the feigned anger represented.

ENERGY USED, ENERGY WASTED

Generalized or free-floating anger, built up like a head of steam, may be converted into energy that, once released, propels us into motion. We may expend such anger in behalf of our own ambitions and need to achieve. Or we may release it in the form of energy spent in behalf of other people, causes, or issues outside ourselves. Some of us can defend with considerable force injustices toward our friends, even strangers, but may feel unable to express anger for injustices toward ourselves. In defending others we are less likely to be subjected to personal attack, less likely to feel guilt since our anger is more easily justified to ourselves and sanctioned by others. Out of anger some of us become crusaders. This is not to suggest that the roots of our convictions and our support of causes always are based in anger, but that they sometimes are, and that such uses of anger may be constructive.

We may believe that we are deriving energy from our anger and using it in behalf of ourselves only to find out that we are wasting energy and using anger in self-defeating ways. I once worked with a young man, a college junior, who was considerably overweight and angry at the world. He railed in anger about his professors and his parents, and fought against the ways he thought they wanted to control him. After several sessions spent working on his overweight and his difficulty coming to terms with people around him and with himself, he came into my office seething with anger.

"I am burned up," he began. "My mother came to see me this weekend. She obviously was glad to see me, and I didn't really mind seeing her." He related incidents of the visit—places they had gone and things they had done—and finally he blurted out, "But what really burned me up was that when she got ready to leave she hugged me and said, 'Take care of my little fat boy.' "

He puffed up like a pouter pigeon and added, "All I can do is get mad!" He paused for a minute or two, looked up, and with a note of resignation in his voice

69

said, as though talking to himself more than to me, "What a pitiful way to be. All I can do is be mad. What a sorry substitute for doing more." He was making the discovery that his anger was sapping his energy, was blocking his potential for learning new ways to relate to his parents and to cope with his own life condition. He had been using his anger against himself while believing that he was using it to defend himself against the world.

ANGER LOCKED IN

We may turn anger outward on others and let it consume our energies as we deny our capacity for coping with life's problems. Or we may hold it in and perhaps lose touch with it and with feelings that may be under it. In overcontrolling anger and monitoring ourselves too rigidly, we restrict our freedom of expression and shut off our spontaneity.

Sometimes our anger builds up into a rage so overwhelming that words cannot express it, cannot be spoken. The body aches with tension, as though the rage is locked into the muscles. When the words become blocked and the feelings become locked, we may need help in loosening up and letting out what is there.

Jeff, a pharmacist in his early thirties, told us in the therapy group, "I feel like a time bomb set to go off. I don't know what it is or what to do about it." He was asked to listen, to sense what he felt, and to try for a word that might partially fit. He paused for a few seconds and then said in a low, steady, controlled voice, "Rage!" He was asked to close his eyes and imagine a scene, perhaps one with someone else in it, from a time in his life when he felt anger or rage. The following is from the dialogue of Jeff's fantasy scene.

"I am a boy and am in the woodshed at my father's farm." Jeff is sitting on a cushion on the floor. His head, back against the wall, gives the impression that he is looking up, even though his eyes are closed. He continues, "I have a metal bar in my hands and am backed up against the wall away from the door. The bar is raised to strike. Dad is standing in front of me." Jeff pauses and then continues, "He is facing me . . . I am telling him not to touch me. He tries to calm me down." Jeff pauses again. "I am about to explode. I tell him again that he must not touch me. I'm afraid that I will hurt him if he does."

Jeff is asked to look at his father's eyes as calmly as he can. Then he is told, "If you feel safe enough picture yourself dropping the bar slowly or handing it to your father." His physical posture relaxes a bit. "I am feeling calmer now and am throwing the bar aside." Now he is asked, "Watch your father's face and respond to him in whatever way you wish." In his fantasy he moves slowly to his father and embraces him, without anger, without fear. Tears course down his face.

A few minutes later, Jeff shared more of what he felt at the moment in his fantasy scene. "I never realized that I felt so much rage toward my father. But what made me so angry was my fear of him. I'm not sure why I was so afraid. And when I embraced him I realized that I also was feeling intense love for him, that I wanted to have him love me. Then I started crying and felt relief. My anger dissolved and with it went the fear. In its place came feelings of warmth. I feel alive and awake after feeling numb for a week."

A week after this incident Jeff had a visit from his father. "My father came unexpectedly to visit my older son who was in the hospital with a broken leg," Jeff told us. "That weekend I was especially curious about what he was like. My interest in him, and the way I actually listened, must have been strange for him. For the first time—surely this is not true, and yet it seems so—I saw him as another person separate and apart from me. He seemed to enjoy our talk and told me a lot about himself, including his upcoming retirement and plans for the future. What a nice visit it was!"

Jeff plunged into some terrifying feelings and, as a consequence, sorted out some of the rage, the fear, and his need for love. Expressing anger and fear, even with support and encouragement, may be painful. Its release, however, can bring relief and can open doors to other feelings, sometimes to intimacy and love. We are incapable of intimacy and deep expressions of love when consumed with anger. Our energies are drained by the demands for control that the anger makes.

INVITING THE ANGER WE FEAR

We may evoke anger in others while declaring that we are afraid of it, do not want it, cannot handle it. At the same time we may use their anger to perpetuate our own, which also is bothersome. Donna, in her early twenties and now in a therapy group, needed very much to be treated tenderly and lovingly. Although she desperately wanted love, she felt so unlovable that she could hardly imagine anyone caring for her. What she most expected from others was rejection and anger. For years she had experienced a great deal of both and had never learned how to cope with them. Without fully understanding it, Donna had gotten into a systematic and self-defeating trap. She often became the victimizer and the victim, the target for rejection and anger, proving that her fears were justified—her own self-fulfilling prophecy.

Here is an example of·how she triggered in others the anger that she feared, and, in the process, fed her own anger. She invited members of the group to tell how they saw her when she was unable or unwilling to hear their responses. Her tone of voice, drooping body posture, and frightened facial expression said, "Handle with care. I am afraid and fragile." In anguish, but with some intent to shock, she referred to herself as an open, raw, and bleeding wound. Reactions to her were: "You describe your feelings so vividly, so tersely, that I become frightened." "You ask for something that I don't know how to give. You scare me."

Donna felt rejected. Defensively then, with eyes flashing, she hit back, "Knowing that I'm drowning, you don't even try to save me!" She was trying to cope with her fear through anger. As she later put it, "My angry slaps defend me against hurt." Yet with such slaps she evoked anger in others. She then interpreted their anger as further rejection and so the pattern continued in a circle. To break out of this cycle, Donna needed to express her fears more directly and in less overwhelming ways so that others could hear. She also needed to sort out and express her anger in clearer terms, instead of, as she once said, "dumping buckets of fears, anger, and hurt all mixed up in confusion into the laps of others."

Other members of the group eventually were able to help. As they began to listen and to understand her hurt and the fear beyond her anger, they had less need to listen and to respond with their own fear and anger. They were less vulnerable to becoming ensnared in Donna's trap and, consequently, were more able to feel a desire to express tenderness and affection, as well as to respond to her in other sensitive ways. As Donna listened to expressions of warmth from others and as others experienced their desire for relationships with her, the anger, fear, and hurt subsided. Responses to her made out of pity or only out of a need to help did not benefit her. Overtures lacking genuineness were taken as further evidence that no one could care for her; they tended to confirm once again her fear of rejection. Significant growth-producing help came only from persons who could get free from her entrapment and who felt a natural desire to reach out to her.

SETTING ANGER FREE

Anger is an emotion that can bring fear as well as cover it up. We may fear that, once out of control, our anger will cause us to become irrational and possibly disintegrate. We may fear that we will become violent and bring destruction to ourselves and others. We may fear that we will provoke anger and violence in someone else.

Anger is an emotion that may bring hurt and suffering, both when we feel it and when we are its target. Pent-up anger may lead to headaches, stomach aches, body tensions, and other physical discomfort. Anger pushed back may bring on depression, despair, and hopelessness. Anger frozen into a revengeful rage becomes corrosive to our inner life and to our life with others. Sustained anger distances us from one another and brings loneliness and alienation. We cannot live as separate persons with separate identities without some distance and isolation. Neither can we live in angry isolation.

I may bury my anger deeply within, like sinking a sealed capsule to the bottom of the sea where it is hard to find, hard to open. But encapsulated anger seeps out. Feelings of discomfort arise within me, and I behave in ways to control them. I cannot control my behavior completely and am haunted by the prospect that the encapsulated anger may explode or in other ways get out and do harm. My best chance for living with myself and with others comes from opening up the capsules of anger and from learning to keep them open.

I need to learn to express anger in small doses, to express it indirectly, to take step-by-step risks in discovering its limits and perhaps the limits of my rage and potential violence. I may thus be able to learn how to reduce the control and dominance anger may have over me. Most of us have deep, internal, almost automatic limits that we can discover once we risk feeling and knowing the depths and consequences of our anger, even to the point of feeling out of control. In facing and knowing my own anger I can minimize its mystery, its strange and often impulsive influences, and its power to dominate and to destroy.

I can never eliminate the power of my anger to hurt. Another person's vulnerability to feel hurt through my anger, like a person's vulnerability to feel hurt through being loved, is a risk inherent in giving up rigid controls over our anger to keep it from becoming encased. The risk of hurt, then, is a condition necessary for letting anger out, for discovering fresh feelings and emotions locked in by the anger, and for renewing and revitalizing our relationships with one another. The other alternative I can see is to encapsulate it and thereby encapsulate an important part of ourselves with it.

6. Fear Mingled
with Hurt

Lessening our fears and easing our hurt are so much a part of life each day that they often go unnoticed. Common ways of attempting to cope with these feelings involve efforts and often ingenious strategies to control ourselves and people and situations around us. We often do need to restrain our behavior. The consequences of overcontrol, however, are tantamount to psychological shutdowns. Sometimes shutdowns are necessary, in crises perhaps, when our emotional reactions inundate us. At such times we may be unable to withstand the bombardment of our senses and the multiplicity of feelings jarred loose. Later, however, we may be able to return to the experience, to recapture some of our feelings, and to sort them out.

IMPRISONED IN FEAR

Most dreaded among our fears are those that we cannot identify, those that have no faces and no names. We may become paralyzed with fears because we feel unable to know them. We may have such need to over-protect ourselves from them, like guarding against the possibilities of anger and hurt, that we become excessively cautious and overly controlled. We can become so fearful of the risks of living and of knowing ourselves that we become psychological prisoners, being both inmate and guard.

Fortunately, we have ways to make many of our fears knowable, ways to test them against realities of day-to-day experiences. We may have rough guides that tell us that some of our fears are real and potentially dangerous, that some are irrational and bothersome but still understandable, and that still others are vague and less well known.

Our anger can turn into vague and irrational fears. We may, for example, have suffered experiences that led us to believe that we would be abandoned if we were to express our anger to those we love. In self-protection we then may have suppressed it. Eventually, anger held back may become a sword turned toward ourselves, a weapon of terror as the anger becomes less accessible, more unknown, secret. Sensing terror, we may go to extreme lengths in controlling our behavior. We may become phobic, that is, irrationally fearful, and displace our fears on other people and objects, and become obsessed with controlling our behavior in a multitude of ways. We stand guard over inner feelings presumed to be dangerous and fearful, even though we may not know what they are—only that we must contain them.

The fear of loss of control over our behavior and our life situation can become pervasive. The need for excessive control may lead us to remove ourselves from involvement with other people and from situations we cannot control. This may be the worst of alternatives, since it lessens our ability to know what we feel and who we are. Detachment, out of fear, deprives us of the relationships and intimacy that may be antidotes against fear. Our withdrawal from relationships may deaden us, dry us up emotionally. When fear sets in, our ability to care suffers. What may be needed then, is help in some manner to reduce the fear, to take small risks in relating to others and in experiencing some degree of nourishment that others can give.

The fear of intimacy, of letting people get too close to us, may stem from the belief that we may be liked at the moment, but rejected later when others get to know us better. Such a fear may stem from our belief that we are unlovable. If I have built a defensive structure and patterns of behavior on the belief that people are not to be trusted nor allowed to come in too close for whatever reason, I may experience anxiety, even disorientation, when someone loves me in ways that I find hard to deny. As strange as it may seem, some of us may need assistance in learning to receive love in small doses. We may understand readily that rejection and anger can be hurtful, and we are likely to have sturdy defenses for dealing with such reactions. We may even invite anger and rejection to keep our defenses intact, as was illustrated in the preceding chapter by the description of Donna's behavior. But if we are unaccustomed to intimacy and love, indeed quite fearful of it, we may not be prepared to handle closeness to others. While love and intimacy are nourishing and essential to growth and happiness, they also may be fearful, even devastating, to someone whose defensive structure is not geared to handle them.

FEAR OF WHAT MIGHT BE THERE

All of us know things about ourselves that we want to keep from others for fear of disapproval and rejection. There also may be things about us that we need to keep secret from ourselves because they are too fearful to face. Yet we may wonder what it would be like to taste and live with the worst, the most fearful, within us. We may wonder also how our fears and what we consider weak and unacceptable within us may be seen and used by someone else, should they discover *what we are really like*. If our fears become known, others may dislike and devalue us. They may try to use what they know about us to hurt or to control us. As mentioned earlier, to protect ourselves we may hold a tight rein on our behavior to keep ourselves and our relationships with others under control.

Molly, a professional woman in her late thirties, entered with both fear and hopeful anticipation a therapeutic group with eleven other people. To use her words, "I was tired of protecting myself and hiding problems that were becoming too big for me to handle in my life. I needed something more in dealing with people than my usual nice-understanding-interested-woman and my parent roles which were getting more and more unsatisfactory." While needing to unburden herself from some of her fear and to reduce the intense pain and anxiety, Molly also needed to guard her actions and to "look good" to other group members.

In the group she was especially considerate of others, almost deferent. She invited others to express their views, and was inclined to protect anyone who was mildly criticized by saying such things as "I understand" ... "Sometimes I'm like that" ... "Many people feel that way." By generalizing situations she,

79

in effect, denied or minimized their importance to others. In the group she smiled a lot, complimented people enthusiastically, and conveyed wide-eyed interest in each exchange. Her behavior was not unlike day-to-day behavior in which many of us engage. Several members of the group, however, began to pick up double meanings in Molly's messages. One was, "I am uncomfortable being older than others here and wonder if I will fit in." Another was, "I am older, more experienced, probably wiser, and expect my views to carry more weight." Her uneasy laughter and tendency to smooth over differences were seen as both sensitivity and fear.

Group members began to give Molly their impressions of what she was doing: "You don't let us know you." "You sneak away by talking about your children." "You don't seem to be coming through as a real person." Molly felt hurt and, as she put it, "bewildered by this, but still tried hard to handle myself and stay in control."

"I felt so rejected," she wrote later. "I had begun to think about how many times I had felt that life had rejected me and that I had never faced that fact. The death of my husband and not establishing another relationship left me in loneliness. I was so unhappy!" Molly felt torn between withdrawing from the group and taking further risks by sharing some of her fears, thus hoping to learn more about the unknown fears she felt that she was controlling.

Molly felt such intense pain that she decided she had little to lose. Often our fear and hurt must increase and even reach intolerable levels before we dare risk confronting them. Molly plunged in. She told the group that she became panic-stricken when on a bus, in a plane, or in a car with someone else driving—in any situation in which she did not have control over the vehicle. She felt similarly panicked if she momentarily could not find the keys to her car when away from home. She needed the security of control, the feeling that she "never must depend on others for what I need." She looked at the floor and muttered, almost inaudibly, "It is so bad . . . so bad. . . ." Tears began to course down her face. Deep sobs came to the surface. The sobs settled into the steady cry of a small child. She held her face in her hands. Several minutes later she stopped crying but continued to cover her face with her hands. Softly she said, "I am so ashamed. I cannot look at anyone."

I moved from her side to face her and held my hands, palms exposed, a few inches from her face and said, "Molly, imagine that my hands are a mirror. Maybe it would help if you would look at yourself in this mirror and see what that feels like."

She raised her head, looked at my hands and began to talk to herself. "Molly, you bad, bad little girl! Shame, shame, shame! You're so bad, so bad! How could you be so bad?" Members of the group moved in to be close to Molly but did not touch her. Molly continued in tones more tender. "You poor child. You poor lonely child." She crossed her arms, placing a hand on each of her shoulders as though comforting herself. She closed her eyes again and continued to hold herself. She looked as though a burden had been lifted.

Molly's description of the incident shortly after tells some of its meaning for her. "Sitting in the middle of the room, crying like a six-year-old child and saying things that bypassed my head was something I had never experienced before. The shock of not controlling myself and acting in that manner, and my reactions to that image of myself in the mirror were unbelievable. The realization that I had a façade all of these years and did not know it! The whole episode was mind-blowing.

"Being able to open up to my private fears and discovering that whatever they are, no matter how shameful, they could be understood and that people could care was a tremendously important discovery. Afterwards, I could not get the experience out of my mind. I kept going back over it and crying again over and over to myself. I cherished that child and wept over the new awareness of myself and the sorrow of past years. Being able to own up to the loneliness I had felt for such a long time and not having to feel ashamed, I wept for the years I have wasted, for the years of not being in touch with myself, years that could have been much richer."

Later she said, "For days now I have felt such a glow, such an openness to myself. The realization came and was so long in coming. It was that I needed to control myself out of the fear that something inside me or something in other people might take me over. Then out of the fear, I might get lost somehow."

Molly's risk in exploring her unkown fears was indeed painful. Her feelings of shame and loneliness and her tears of sadness came bubbling out beyond her control in her little girl sobs and crying. Once she could express and own the feelings of the little girl within her, she could experience them—the sadness, loneliness, fears, and tears—as an adult. The little girl and the woman then could become one. Molly's moving experience became possible in relationships with others who could hold before her the mirrors of her double messages, the mirror of the face and feelings of a little girl, and finally a mirror reflecting a more spontaneous, self-confident woman who was less afraid and more aware of her fears.

What Molly discovered and what many of us learn and perhaps have to relearn again and again is that what we find within ourselves is seldom, if ever, so awesome as the fear of what we suspect might be there.

It is sensing and not facing the pain and the fear that are far worse than knowing and facing whatever is there.

FREEDOM TO FALL APART

We use a variety of experiences to touch and sort out our feelings—work, play, hobbies, sports, travel, sometimes with others, sometimes alone. We may find that religion, music, literature, or certain aesthetic experiences add depth and breadth to our emotions and heighten our sense of aliveness. Counseling and psychotherapy and intensive therapeutic groups are special situations in which we can search out both conscious and unconscious feelings within us. We may find a climate in which to reexperience and face our fears, to name them, to live through them, to discover that we can survive them. Once we have faced the depths of our fears and have survived panic, we may discover that they lose their grip on us, that we no longer need to expend energy constantly to stand guard over ourselves lest we pop out of control or lose ourselves in some unknown way.

At times we may risk disengaging from life, risk coming apart and going out of control, in the hope that we can come back together again and feel more whole, less need for control. Taking such a risk gives us no guarantee that our defensive controls will be replaced with something better. The letting down of defenses and the giving up of control often are followed by periods in which we feel too flexible, too fluid, too shaky in terms of how to act. Such out-of-control feelings can be frightening. We may feel undefined as persons. We need time and opportunities to try new ways of coping, relating to others, and looking at ourselves. We may find ourselves searching for our own unique paths to wholeness and to self-discovery. Such searching allows us to come apart psychologically, to reshuffle our feelings, including our fears, and to come back together in a more integrated fashion. Once in a while, new ways of behaving come suddenly and unexpectedly, but more often they come at a snail's pace.

MORE HURT OR PROMISED JOY

In coming to terms with our fears and in risking new behavior we may feel emotionally raw and easily hurt. Our usual ways of defending ourselves against hurt may be suspended. In looking and listening deeply within ourselves to find out what is there, we may come upon old wounds not fully healed and buried grief that has gone unexpressed. We may feel conflict and be puzzled over whether to uncover and examine old pain and grief or to tuck them away again. Either step is a risk. We can feel some safety in the knowledge that, having lived with hurt locked up, we can continue to do so, but we also may feel uneasy and unfinished in having sealed off a part of ourselves. To unlock and open ourselves up to the hurt, we risk feeling more pain and we risk finding no resolution. Then again, we may find relief and strength in facing ourselves as well as a sense of becoming fuller, richer persons.

Letting out our psychological pain, whether it is rooted in past or present experiences, usually involves sharing with others and facing the uncertainties of whether or not we will be understood and accepted. In sharing our hurt and vulnerability, we may be bringing ourselves more fully into relationships with both the promises of joy and the possibilities of further hurt thus being increased. We may discover that in loving someone and being loved, like espousing a conviction held deeply, we are exposing ourselves to others in ways that can be painful.

RETREAT FROM HURT

A concern of mine and of some of the people with whom I work is that too frequently we do not let someone else know when we feel vulnerable and hurt. I may feel embarrassed, ashamed, weak, and fearful of being misunderstood, and hold the pain back or block it out. I even may hold back for fear that someone may understand me and *care too much*. Such care and understanding may be so supportive and strong that I break open to still greater hurt somewhere inside.

No doubt many of us often hide our hurt for reasons that are good in our eyes. But sometimes we may listen sensitively to ourselves, get in touch with the hurt, even want to share, but then retreat from it. The hurt itself may drive us away. Let me illustrate.

A young man in a therapy group was feeling sad as he discussed his failures as a boy to get the love and affection he still missed from his parents. Paul, a young lawyer sitting across the room, began remembering incidents from his boyhood. He felt the pain of his mother's rejection and the loneliness of feeling left out while the other boys played. He was absorbed in those earlier feelings when he told the group, "I still feel the terrible hurt as I think about walking across the park and sitting alone on the bench there. I always went to that bench. Even now it represents most of the incurable loneliness and pain I felt as a boy."

Paul's eyes were fixed on the floor in the center of the room. His face was grim. He glanced up at me and then at a woman sitting on his right. Quickly his face became a frozen grin.

"What happened?" I asked. "You seemed to leave yourself and your feelings stranded in that instant."

"I feel silly. All that's not important any more, " he replied as he straightened up and replaced the grin with an expression of controlled detachment.

Paul had truly begun to listen to the hurt that he felt. Suddenly, he moved, psychologically speaking, from being in touch with what was on the inside to a more detached position on the outside. He then looked at himself as a judge perched above and over his shoulder. In self-consciousness and disapproval of his feelings, he withdrew, covering up his hurt. He did that often. As a consequence, he carried the hurt and loneliness and rarely let them out.

What Paul experienced next came as a surprise. In discussing what had happened and how he had moved away from his hurt, he found out that the eight other people in the room had stayed with him in his hurt. No one censored him for sidestepping it, but they let him know that they thought his feelings as a boy and now as a man were important and not at all silly. Members of the group did not join him in his retreat from the hurt, and Paul felt alone again. He felt detached from himself and from others in the room, just as he had felt as a boy. He had made sure of it as we watched him.

After a few weeks Paul began to stay in touch with his hurt for longer periods of time. With support from other group members he could risk letting his hurt be felt and then shared. And, as often happens, it recurred less frequently and lost some of its sting. Learning to allow the hurt also lessened the fright that usually accompanied it—the fright that he would look silly and be rejected and that the pain would get worse and worse and finally overpower him.

RETURN FROM THE HURT

Some of us seem to know and others among us can learn how to let out our hurt, how to let others be with us, and how to be with them in moments of deep sadness, loneliness, and psychological pain. Too, we can learn to receive the sensitive care, the love, and the support that others can give. A frequent problem, however, is that when we are in pain and grief we may receive too much support too early from others. In this way we are prevented from experiencing the fullness and the depth of the hurt, an experience necessary to discover that we can endure it and derive strength from it. We are more likely to experience the depths of our sadness, our hurt, our loneliness if we are cared for in ways that do not minimize or disallow our feelings, even though others might feel relief if we did not feel so deeply.

Sometimes our hurt, like our fear and our anger, may get cut loose from its moorings. We may feel it but not know where it is coming from or where it is connected. We may have pushed back the experience with which the pain is associated. The reason we push back some experiences, of course, is that they are too painful or threatening. We may not want to remember them. If we decide to risk uncovering and expressing painful emotions, we may discover how closely we can get to ourselves, how unguarded we can become, and how deeply others can be with us in our hurt.

"I am feeling uncomfortable, tight, and for some reason very sad." Anna, a psychologist in a group training workshop, was talking about how she felt at that moment. As soon as she acknowledged her sadness, she began to cry softly.

I had been watching her and after a few seconds asked gently, "Is it something you want to talk about, Anna?" She opened her eyes and looked up. She had been in her own private world. She did not know what she was sad about but decided to talk about whatever came to mind to see what she might come upon. She recounted to the group that she felt shaken up from seeing two girls lying in the street earlier in the morning, apparently hit and injured by a car. People had gathered and had covered them up while waiting for the ambulance and police. She had been in such a hurry that she had momentarily forgotten that.

Another incident of the morning was on her mind. On her way to the workshop session, she had dropped off a six-year-old girl, a neighbor's daughter, at the child's grandmother's house. While riding in the car the child mentioned how scared she had been a few days ago because a little friend of hers "almost drowned." Anna felt uneasy. She knew that the little girl's friend had drowned and could not be revived at the hospital. She found herself saying over and over to herself in the car, "They never told her. They never told her." Now, in the workshop group, she was recalling this incident and her sadness for the little girl.

Anna remembered that two years ago her son was lost at Disneyworld near a lake and she feared that he had drowned. Fortunately he had not. She talked about how much she missed her children who were visiting her family in another city. All of these certainly were incidents about which to feel sadness. A member of the workshop group went over and hugged Anna. She stopped crying. The hug, well-intended and supportive, interrupted Anna as she explored her hurt. She said that she had nothing more she wanted to say, that she was finished. Still, she looked sad. Her eyes seemed to be questioning and searching, as though seeking some missing link. She sat in silence. No one in the group spoke to break the silence.

After two or three minutes a look of awareness flashed across Anna's face. The words "They never told *her*" that she had repeated earlier became "They never told *me*. They never told *me!*" She had said those same words several years back one day in October when she was in her teens and had read in the newspaper that her grandmother had died. She had loved her grandmother very much, and felt so close to her. Mamapepa, she called her. Her Mamapepa was born in Mexico.

Anna related how numbed she felt with anger toward her father for not telling her. Her mother was not present at the time. Her father explained that he had wanted her to feel that she had her Mamapepa one more day. She later found out how terribly painful it had been for him to talk to her about it. She had not gotten to attend her grandmother's funeral. Now, sitting in the room, Anna knew what her deep gnawing sadness was about. She sat alone, again in tears and sadness, mourning the loss of her grandmother that day in October.

"Would you like to say something to your grandmother, Anna?" I asked.

"Yes."

"Close your eyes and see if you can picture the last time you saw her." Pause. "Are you with her?"

"We are in her bedroom. She is in her bed and I am sitting on the edge of it." Anna's voice was tender. She continued, "She looks so thin and tired. It's her eyes. Her eyes want to say something."

"What is it?"

"She is saying, 'I am very tired, my Anna, and I want to go rest.'" Anna put her hand over her mouth as if to hold back a gasp. She then said, "She is telling me she's ready to die."

"What do you want to say to her?"

"Please, please don't leave me, Mamapepa. I need you."

"Maybe, Anna," I suggested, "you're the person she needs to say this to."

"Yes, she says that I'm the only one. She knows I'll understand. She has much trust and faith in me. I want to tell her. 'Gracias.'"

"Yes, speak to her in Spanish."

"Yo te amo mucho, Mamapepa, y gracias por todo el cariño que me has dado." [I love you very much, Mamapepa, and thank you for all the love you have given me.] Anna's eyes remained closed, and she leaned forward as though to make certain her grandmother would hear her soft voice.

"What is she saying back to you, Anna?"

" 'You have been the joy and pleasure in my life, my Anna, but I want to rest. I am tired . . . so tired.' "

Anna then spoke again to her grandmother. *"Mamapepa, me enseñaste muchisimo. . . . Siempre te recordaré, y guardaré como un tesora tantas memorias involvidables de nuestro amor eterno."* [Mamapepa, you have taught me so much.] Pause. [I will remember you always, and keep like a treasure so many unforgettable memories of our eternal love.] Many seconds passed.

"Anna, when you are ready, see if you can tell her goodbye." Anna slowly extended her arms with palms down as though touching her grandmother.

She said simply and lovingly, *"Adios, Mamapepa, adios."* She held her face in her hands and softly wept. I wept quietly with her.

After some time passed, I suggested, "Go someplace, if you wish, in your grandmother's house where you can be alone to cry."

"Yes, I need to do that," Anna replied. She continued to weep softly.

I placed a pillow in front of her. She held it in her arms. She then stretched out on the floor and held the pillow against her cheek as she cried.

Minutes later Anna opened her eyes and said, "I feel unburdened and quite peaceful now."

And then, to let us know more of what happened, she said, "I walked into the back bedroom of my grandmother's house. I cried and cried and cried. Oh, the pain! My whole body hurt. My stomach hurt. I held the pillow tightly and imagined my grandmother was holding me. I cried for her and I cried for me. I had lost that warm, safe place to go when no one else understood me. So I cried some more."

I brim with appreciation, compassion, and wonder for Anna and people like her who search out and then let out their hurt in ways that complete and enrich them. They represent eloquently our humanity, our resilience, and our power for renewal. They help me to hit the bottom of my own sadness and hurt and then to get up again, feeling that the roots of my strength are deep and nourishing. During moments like those with Anna I feel a deep sense of communion. I also feel a deep sense of loneliness in my own separateness. Embracing both—communion and separateness—while remaining present to listen to others and to ourselves is surely something to be prized if our lives and relationships are to run deep.

7. Messages of Silence

Deeper meanings are sometimes not easily expressed or heard in words. When words clutter, silence may carry the meaning. The deeper meaning is the experience, the feeling, the thing in itself. Carl Rogers wrote in the preface of one of his books: "If one wishes to give . . . real meaning he should put his hand over his mouth and *point*."[1] Special moments in our relationships may come when we are with one another as though pointing in silence. Our words come from silence and return there. Our silences and our words punctuate one another and give continuity to our language. "If there were no gaps between our words," writes R. P. Blackmur, ". . . we should never find our thoughts or recognize the thoughts of others."[2]

We may be with one another through the expression of words and then continue together in silence. But at some point we may lose contact in silence, just as we do in words. Our silences may become ambiguous, cloudy, without clear meaning. When they endure beyond comprehension, they may need to be broken with another response—a word, gesture, eyes meeting and signaling meaning.

OUR USES OF SILENCE

If you and I break a dialogue to return to silence, what decisions do we make about how we are listening and being with one another? My silence might be a withdrawal from you, a desire to relate to you without words, or a desire to wait quietly for awhile. What will you hear? Will your eyes listen, will they watch for the silent language of the body? You might feel shut off from me and listen to your own thoughts and feelings. Most likely something is happening within each of us. Neutrality in our silences is unlikely. Your inner dialogue in silence may be a continuation of our dialogue in words. Mine may center on something else. Whatever is happening, our silence may represent how we want to be in relationship for the moment.

If we discover the common and unique uses and meanings of silences in our relationships we can understand and distinguish among them. I may use silence to be seen as enigmatic. Your silence may be an invitation for me to infer your meaning or to project my own. Meaning imposed upon your silence may distort its nature and create a gap in our understanding. Another gap in understanding may occur if, while you talk, you impose only your interpretation of what my silent listening means. I may feel open and accepting; you may construe my silence as closed and rejecting.

93

Projections onto silences by both of us may lead to a kind of dual distortion.

Silence may be used to convey impressions without having to acknowledge responsibility for them. The politician's "No comment" may be followed by silence and nonverbal cues—a knowing smile, a glance that promises more, a look that affirms or denies. Messages may come in silence, and the meanings may be carried through body language—expressions of the face, particularly the mouth and eyes, the posture of the shoulders, the positioning of the arms and hands.

Moods of Silence

"There are, of course, different kinds of silence," writes the psychoanalyst Theodor Reik. "We speak of a cold, oppressive, defiant, disapproving or condemning, as well as a calming, approving, humble, excusing silence. Silence can be...an expression of quiet sympathy or intense hate. To be silent with a person may mean that we feel quite in agreement with him or that every possibility of agreement is excluded."[3] Silence may say, I am waiting to hear, or I am not listening. It may mean meditation, peace, serenity; it may mean turmoil, conflict, despair. A silence might be pleasurable or painful; it might be an approach to action or it might be an avoidance of thoughts, feelings, words. One of Theodor Reik's patients, "who had interrupted her report with a long pause, which she tried in vain to break by talking about indifferent things, fell back into a long silence. It was obvious that she did not want to talk about a certain experience the memory of which was accompanied by feelings of grief. Finally she said, 'Let's be silent about something else.' "[4]

Silence may be an instrument of punishment that whips you into submission, that stirs your guilt, that drives a wedge to split you off from others. Tanya, twelve, did not speak to her father after he separated from her mother. The punishment was severe for him, and for her. He passed through guilt to despair during her silence and then to a disquieting resignation that all he could do was wait and wonder how long. A year later her silence was broken. He stopped by the house to say goodbye to his other children before moving to another state. Tanya could hold out no longer. She clutched her father's waist and buried her face in his chest. She burst into torrential tears. Her sobs carried sadness and relief. She could touch and talk with him once more.

Invitations in Silence

Our silences may be invitations for others to look at us, to believe that we are somebody without our having to tell or to show them. Our words may be a similar invitation. And the opposite may be true. Our silences and words may say, "Keep away."

At the beginning of the therapy group Jessica was silent. Hers was a busy silence. In reflecting on it later, she said, "I was quiet in an unknown and potentially dangerous place. I wrote a lot of notes, sometimes to avoid feeling what others felt, sometimes to avoid my own feelings, always to keep attention away from me. I was extremely busy. In a strange way, in being silent I was fighting to keep people away, but I was also fighting my own desire to be noticed."

When Jessica began to talk more in the group she, in her words, "came across as dramatic, motherly, gossipy, and talked so much that I discovered that I kept people away more by talking than I did in my silence." Later she felt safer and allowed herself to move closer to others, in both her silences and her words.

Silence can become a satisfying refuge from having to talk, from having to be noticed, or from having to appear brilliant, witty, and in control. In groups the norm often is to be comfortable speaking up, expressing what is on your mind or what you feel. An equally important norm is the freedom to be silent. The satisfaction of sitting silently while feeling present to oneself and others has a different tone than the silence invoked out of fear of criticism or fear of sounding like a fool. The silence of the husband or wife who listens pridefully to his or her spouse has a flavor different from the silence of retreat from domination.

When Silence Stares

In silence our eyes may carry the message. We speak of caring eyes, gentle eyes, eyes of jealousy, hatred, and rage. The attention we give others with our eyes may bring them closer or hold them back. In a human relations training group, Ben was confronted by members about what they called his "silent stare." He had no idea that it was putting them off. He thought that "it pulled [him] closer" to them. Instead they looked away to avoid feelings of self-consciousness from such close scrutiny and out of fear of being impaled by his stares.

At the close of a series of counseling sessions with a young man, we were looking back attempting to evaluate the experience. I was relatively new in the profession and wanted to get impressions that might be useful. The reaction that I remember now, many years later, is that he said, "You sometimes looked at me too much when we were silent." He continued, "The more you looked, the more silent it became, and finally it became so silent that my words became frozen. All I could do was wiggle."

Elements in Silence

Silences may be time-oriented. My silence in the moment may take me to the past; yours may take you to the future. To wait in silent expectation for an answer or a response from someone else may magnify the moment and put time in slow motion. Or to be caught up in our own reveries may be to suspend time, lose it, rule it out for minutes or hours.

A shared silence may reflect different degrees of intensity. Your silence may be a spotlight to focus vividly on a thought or feeling; mine may dim and shade or take out of focus what I am feeling.

The same silence may be freeing or restricting. In silence you may be free to wander from idea to idea, from feeling to feeling without boundaries, while I may be encapsulated in a thought or feeling.

Silence may be understood in terms of whose it is, who "caused it." It might be yours or mine, depending on who spoke last, the tone used, how the words were punctuated, what is expected.

Silence may be a time for review and synthesis of what we think and feel, what the words mean in all the ways they can have meaning.

BRIEF SCENARIOS IN SILENCE

The context of our silence—the setting, the people, how we know and see one another, and the mixture of these—sets the tone and adds meaning. Silence among strangers feels and sounds different from silence among friends. Silence among friends at a cocktail party sounds different from silence among friends at church, in class, or at the park. Silence among strangers in a meeting room waiting for the therapy group to begin changes in quality when the therapist or group leader walks into the room. And each subsequent silence of the group takes on its own special meaning for individuals and for the group as a whole.

In the words of one group member, Maggie, the silences come "in many flavors." Maggie's flavors are "the fun silence of eyeball games, when I conjecture about people in the group and what they are thinking; the contemplative silence when I'm facing myself and what I am feeling; the frightened silence when I get busy with frenzied activity in order to run away; and the vegetative states of silence and idleness, when I just sit or lie there."

Sherry uses silences early in the group to "divest myself of the trivia swirling around in my head and to look at everyone, to bring to mind what they said last, and to try to figure out where I am with each one." For Dan silences often are a time "to rehearse and evaluate what I want to say. Will I say what I mean? Will I be understood? Accepted? Rejected? Do I really want to say that? Is it all that important? After I have gone through all that, I seldom speak."

Silences may bring out feelings of needing to be responsible: "Oh, no! This silence has gone on too long. Won't someone take responsibility for saying something! Maybe I should. No, what will I say?" Resistance and resentment may be felt: "I'm tired of having to get things started. I'll be damned if I'm going to start it this time. I refuse to say a word until someone else does."

Prolonged silences may make talking difficult. A group member wants to say something, but in the moment before speaking becomes aware that the silence has become pervasive and forbidding. Kate shared an inner dialogue: "I have something I would like to talk about, but it's been so long since someone talked. What I want to say seems trivial. I've let too much time go by. If I say it now, everyone will think it's important, and it's really not that big a deal. Surely somebody with something really important to say will talk if I wait a little longer." The expectation that words in the silence must be significant leads to censoring and then to more silence. The silence then restricts and confines like an invisible cage.

A silence broken may bring relief and then disappointment. Kate's inner dialogue continues: "Oh, I'm so glad that David finally said something. What a relief! But what he said is no more important than what I wanted to say. I'm disappointed that I waited instead of saying it. Maybe next time ... maybe." Or in Dan's words: "A few times I *almost* did say it, did make some observations that later seemed to be just what someone else said. Right on the button! Then I'd kick myself for not having had the guts to say it."

Some silences in therapy groups are used by different individuals to consider what others say and how it relates to them. "I turn it around and look at it this way and that, holding it up to the light. Or, if what is being said is beautiful, I just luxuriate in it, let it soak in." Patricia was speaking of her reaction to silence in the group, and added, "But if I am afraid that I will cry or react in some other way that would be embarrassing, I just sit, controlled and in silence." But sitting in silence is not always calming or protective. When John felt that he should speak up to break a silence, "it became an incoherent buzzing that got louder and louder." For Mary Ann silence sometimes came with "a shock, and all I could hear then was the last sound in the room. Janie, for example, burst out crying with sobs and then wails, and the sheer sound of it pierced my own silent self-involvement. Then suddenly, Janie stopped. I could still hear her as the last sound of my silence. It's often like that. In silence I hear the last sound."

Silence is occasionally a time for discovery. "I deceive myself about listening to others sometimes," Rose said. "Claude spoke of his father's death and I believed that I was listening to him with all my strength;

99

I was immersed in his intense sorrow. Yet, reflecting in silence, I slowly became aware that my tears spilled from my own sorrows. My sense of unity with him was an expression of my own need for closeness as an escape from loneliness. Without realizing it I was busy feeling my own feelings and running from my own fears."

Silence in therapy groups may reduce self-consciousness and free a person from the intruding presence of others. A participant sitting in silence may suddenly begin to talk aloud as though what started in silence is continuing in words. For a moment we may not know whether he is talking only to himself, to others in the group, or to someone not present. Soon, however, his words begin to touch others present, regardless of whether or not he consciously intends for them to do so. Shana caught this flavor of intensity and involvement in a group experience and the quality of listening when she said, "When one of us expresses deep emotions that are happening now, the silence around is like *pure listening*."

The integration of silence as a part of the many languages of a group was described by Linda, who wrote, "As our group matured, ripened, aged, or whatever therapy groups do with time, I found that my running analyses of my silences got fewer and fewer. Finally silence was no longer a separate thing. It had become integrated with me, with others, and with what we said."

FUGITIVE FROM SILENCE

On occasion, Byron, in individual therapy, becomes a fugitive from silence, a runaway from himself through words. He speaks of many feelings, people, and events, all connected somewhere at some level in his own experiences, but disconnected in his expression. The momentum picks up until he seems more anxious, disoriented, out of control, dashing headlong into nowhere. He may need to run hard, psychologically speaking, but he also may need to slow down and stop. If I listen carefully, I may pick out a thread of meaning and let him know what I hear. Feeling slightly heard, he may pause in relief and listen to himself. I may touch his hand, arm, or shoulder and ask him to let himself and his words slow down. He may feel himself coming to another pause. Soon he may be ready to allow silence.

The silence may be a haven where Byron, for a while, can touch himself to allow what is there—fear, anger, jumbled-up conflicts. Soon he may come out of the silence to express himself more satisfactorily in words.

8. Silence and Loneliness

In moments of dialogue with ourselves we may be able to feel our inner conflicts and the torment of being alone and out of touch with ourselves and with the people we love. In such moments we may be able to come to terms with fuller definitions of ourselves, using the knowledge that silent self-examination may yield.

This is not to say that all loneliness is silent or that all silences are lonely. We may feel lonely in the crowd, or accompanied when alone. Similarly, when we sit engulfed in our own silence, we may hear no sounds around us. Or the sounds around and within may clang and bang and beat in our ears in the midst of our silence.

WHEN NO ONE IS THERE

There are periods of being alone and in silence when life inside us seems quiet, but also stirs. There may be a quality of absorption in our inner experiencing that we may relish. We may feel peaceful, satisfied, exhilarated, and whole.

Being alone is not always a choice we have made. We may feel, and indeed be, rejected and abandoned. Circumstances may force us to be alone physically. In our aloneness we may become deeply lonely. When we are alone, whether we feel lonely or not, we may talk to people who are not there and to objects that remain silent. When we are silent, we may have inner dialogues with people, real and imagined, those we love and those we hate. We may conjure up revenge fantasies and speak sharply, admonishing someone who has hurt or angered us, and who is no longer there to speak back. We may talk to the trees, the birds, the flowers, or to the gathering clouds. Aloud and in silence we may express ourselves to people, parts of nature, and assorted objects to release ourselves, share our joy, let out our sadness. Occasionally we may hear replies—conversations in silence.

The poets, artists, and song writers may speak for us with eloquence, passion, or candor. "Hello, walls," laments Willie Nelson in the lonely country folksong. "How did things go for you today? Don't you miss her, since she up and walked away?"[1] The walls are silent. He can have his say—no concern about what comes back.

Silent conversations and songs, and the silent scenes we create and enact, allow us to walk nakedly before ourselves to see and accept what life is and what we wish it to be.

By solitary conversations with objects and with creations of nature, we try to hold onto something more stable and less threatening than people who could hurt

103

us. In our loneliness, animals and plants may become objects for a personalized relationship and may come to symbolize hope. Viktor Frankl[2] describes such a relationship experienced by a young woman who was soon to die in a concentration camp. He writes, "When I talked to her she was cheerful in spite of this knowledge. 'I am grateful that fate has hit me so hard. . . . In my former life I was spoiled and did not take spiritual accomplishments seriously.' Pointing through the window of the hut, she said, 'This tree here is the only friend I have in my loneliness.' Through that window she could see just one branch of a chestnut tree, and on the branch were two blossoms. 'I often talk to this tree,' she said to me. I was startled and didn't quite know how to take her words. Was she delirious? Did she have occasional hallucinations? Anxiously I asked her if the tree replied. 'Yes.' What did it say to her? She answered. 'It said to me, "I am here—I am here—I am life, eternal life".' "

BEYOND THE "ZONE OF SILENCE"

There is a deeper, more isolated and frightening loneliness in silence. "In the Pacific, near the Vancouver Island," writes Theodor Reik, "there is a strange place called the 'Zone of Silence.' Here many ships have been wrecked on the rocks and lie on the bottom of the sea. No siren is powerful enough to warn the captains. No sound from outside can penetrate this zone of silence extending for many miles. A ship in this area is excluded from the noise of the outside world. What we call the repressed material in psychical life can be compared to the 'zone of silence.' "[3]

Fear, loneliness, and isolation may get locked into our zones of silence and become impossible to express. We cannot hear what is there, and no one can hear us. We dare not let them try. Frieda Fromm-Reichmann[4] speaks of a loneliness in silence that is so terrorizing that it cannot be shared. The silent pain and despair become fearful and anxiety-ridden, but the prospect of breaking the silence and exiting from the profound loneliness is even more shattering to contemplate.

We may ridicule the insignificance of superficiality in our language and in our talk. We may get bored with one another through talk of trivialities. If we are depressed, in despair, or in deep states of loneliness, superficial talk may be a way to hang onto whatever reality seems at hand. Routine ventures from our silence may be signals to ourselves that we are alive and can say something to someone, including ourselves.

Fromm-Reichmann[5] refers to the accounts by Christopher Burney, who was held by the Germans for eighteen months in solitary confinement during World War II, and to similar experiences in which persons became so isolated and lived so deeply in the silence of their inner world that only with extreme difficulty and caution could they come out of silence, adjust to the use of words, and reestablish a life with other human beings.

The ability to speak and the ability to be silent and remain in touch with ourselves and with others are terribly important. To become encapsulated in silence and life only in our inner world, no matter how vivid it becomes, is to lose the other side of life, a life with others. And to become entrapped in words as an escape from our inner life is to lose sensitivity to ourselves.

The thought of losing sensitivity brings to mind Viktor Frankl's account of his concentration camp experiences.[6] He described the psychology of the prisoners who were being released and who were allowed to venture from camp. He talked about their efforts to grasp freedom and its reality which had kept hope alive for many years. He wrote: "We came to the meadows full of flowers. We saw and realized that they were there, but we had no feelings about them. The first spark of joy came when we saw a rooster with a tail of multicolored feathers. But it remained only a spark; we did not yet belong to this world.

"In the evening when we all met again in our hut, one said secretly to the other, 'Tell me, were you pleased today?'

"And the other replied, feeling ashamed as he did not know that we all felt similarly, 'Truthfully, no!' We had literally lost the ability to feel pleased and had to relearn it slowly." The prisoners, robbed of their sensitivity, lost the deeply intense and personal meaning that all the grains of life can have.

Ted had not descended so deeply into a silence of loneliness that he could not make ascents and live life with others, but he lived in fear of it. It was a long marathon session of an ongoing intensive group in which members were trying to resolve conflicts that had built up over the weeks. Ted had been quiet all afternoon. He was not alone physically. People were sitting around him; still he seemed to be lost among them. Someone asked if he were bothered about something. As was often the case, he smiled and said, "No, not really." His reply did not satisfy. He looked worried about something and people there wanted to know what it was.

Ted told the group that he lived with a lingering dread of withdrawing so completely that he could never have any human contact again. He feared that he suddenly would enter into a world of his own and shut himself off and everyone else out. Yet the prospect of such a state was not without attraction. He talked in tones of futility. But, on balance, his desire to stay alive emotionally had gathered momentum recently. I asked Ted if he wanted to risk taking a step toward breaking the barrier of fear and isolation. "Yes," he replied after a moment of hesitation. "I must do something."

"Try to allow yourself to take the physical posture that represents what you most fear." I suggested. "Close your eyes and slowly let in whatever feelings occur as you sit there." Sitting on the floor, Ted locked both arms around his legs below the knees and lowered his head to where his eyes could gaze at the floor. Members of the group were invited to take similar positions if they wished as a way of trying to feel with Ted. Whether it would become a flight from life, a small step toward renewal, or an inconsequential activity, I could not know for certain. Ted was asked to let himself feel whatever might come, to float in his feelings from moment to moment, or to allow himself to go blank as he pictured himself in whatever setting he could imagine. There was a pause.

"With your eyes still closed, and holding onto the feelings and scene of the moment, can you share where you are and what you are feeling?" Pause.

"I'm in a dark corner...afraid of the dark...and what might happen to me." His voice was low and quivering. Silence.

"How old are you now in this scene?"

"It's now." Pause. "It's terrifying." Silence.

"Do you want someone with you?"

"No." Ted's teeth began to chatter, and his entire body shook. In a low monotone, "It's cold." A member of the group quickly got a shawl and gently draped it over Ted's shoulders and arms. He wept softly as he shook. His body slackened. The weeping continued. Finally he spoke through his tears. "It's dark. No light at all." Silence.

To offer the possibility of relief and to test for any signs of hope that Ted might feel, I suggested, "There may be one small ray of light if you can see it."

"It's on the ceiling," Ted responded immediately, but his words were drowsy and barely audible. "It's on a spider moving over my head to drop on me." Silence.

"Picture yourself sitting there watching the spider while it watches you." Pause.

"It has moved on now ... no longer notices me." Pause.

Since the ray of light was accepted, I asked, "Is there a window, a door, or an opening anywhere near?"

"Yes, there is a window." Ted had stopped shaking. His voice was a bit stronger. Two or three minutes passed. They seemed like ten stretched to twenty.

"Can you see out the window?"

"There is a garden. No people, a garden ... green grass, trees." Pause. His voice was slightly stronger.

"Do you want to go there, or stay where you are?"

"I need to stay here." Minutes passed. Ted shifted his body and eased the grip around his legs. His eyes remained closed. His head was raised slightly with his chin on his knees.

"Where are you now? What is happening?" The shift of his body suggested such a possibility.

"I'm back home sitting, hiding, between two dressers in the bedroom." Silence.

"How old are you?"

"Twelve." Ted was making contact with earlier experiences and a way of defending himself. His eyes were still closed, but his face was more open. "I am not so afraid now."

"Stay there awhile, and then, if you can, imagine yourself growing bigger and older as you return to your life now." Two or three minutes passed.

"I'm coming back. I'm still not so afraid." There seemed to be a slight edginess in returning.

"When you are ready to come back to this room there are people to be with you." Pause. "If you want to join others here, slowly open your eyes, or let yourself ease over toward either side and someone will be there to hold you." Silence.

Slowly Ted leaned over to his left and Hannah held

him. He lay curled up peacefully in a fetal position. Up to this moment no one had touched him. It was important that he be alone unless he signaled for help or comfort from others. Now he seemed ready. Members of the group moved closer and gently touched him in different ways. There were no efforts to smother him in ways that might detract from his inner experience or take away his control of the situation. A look of serenity came over his face. For weeks he had been aloof, remote, unwilling for anyone to get close to him. His barricades were removed for the moment. He was less lonely, less isolated.

Living or reliving an experience in a guided fantasy in a therapeutic setting is a way of loosening up our emotions, and of making them more accessible, more manageable, and less threatening. Experiencing feelings buried deeply within us opens up possibilities for them to become less distorted so that they can be known and can be endured. Their power over us is diminished.

Often during an intense and moving fantasy, persons apparently on the sidelines and out of the spotlight may get lost in side trips into their own emotions and may have trouble getting back. It was necessary, therefore, that those who were in the experience with Ted share their own ways of being present to him and to themselves. A few individuals did get snared and needed to resolve or relieve conflicted or suspended emotions. Explorations by other participants continued while Ted lay relaxed with his head in Hannah's lap. After awhile he sat up and was asked to look at each member's eyes as a way of making direct contact with them, and of sensing how they felt present to him through their eyes.

Through the fantasy experience Ted had opted to take a step out of his fear that was locked in silence. The hardest steps were the beginning and the end—

letting himself go into the fear and isolation, and later facing others through his eyes. The scenes and dialogues in silence, in fantasy, and in words seemed singularly important for Ted. And they were important in unique ways for others who were there with him.

Members present struggled, first to allow and then to experience Ted's fear and loneliness. And they risked dipping into their own. In silence they seemed to transcend their fears and to discover a bond among one another. A special intimacy was born out of the knowledge that something important had taken place there—something that could not necessarily become fully known and understood by all of them.

A few days later Ted commented on his immersion in the experience. "I keep remembering the night I got into that heavy fantasy experience, and how everyone was really tuned in to me. Toward the end I rolled over into Hannah's lap and everyone came around. When I looked at the faces of those people, I couldn't believe it. There was such love and caring on their faces. I don't think that I have ever seen anything more beautiful or more moving. I just lay back down on the floor and curled up in the feeling. Someone said, 'Look at Ted. Have you ever seen him looking so peaceful?' " Ted then added, "I had died and gone to heaven."

For the moment his was a heaven of peace and love —and silence.

9. The Secret You

As has been illustrated throughout this book, hidden facets of our emotions and behavior are a part of our inner world and may dominate much of our external world. Secrets in themselves are fascinating, intriguing, powerful, and sometimes fearful. Having secrets is inevitable, whether they exhilarate or hurt, isolate or bring intimacy. But only if we learn to listen to our secrets and to uncover them can we know their meaning.

WHAT ARE SECRETS LIKE?

Secrets may be pillars to tie to, like close trusted friends. They may be pieces of the soul; wines that mature with age; raindrops, candy, and ice cream; jewels; marbles once played with and now stored away; special parts of oneself not given. Or they may be traps, obstacles to others, internal weights, time bombs, demons, weapons, or dark boxes.

Secrets can be two-sided: like fire—warm but dangerous; like shadows—here, there, then gone; like the wind—warm and refreshing, then suddenly cold and biting. These are some of the words used to describe secrets by people who recently shared with me the meaning of their secrets.[1]

What are our secrets about? Ambitions; hopes; wishes; sexual feelings that are too strong, too weak, or unfulfilled; loneliness; rejection; weaknesses and inadequacies; powerful and potentially destructive feelings of love, hate, murder, death, embarrassment, shame, and guilt; mixed and complicated feelings about members of our families.

Our secret ambitions and hopes often drive us. We may scrutinize the lives of great men and women in history to uncover the secrets they used to move themselves into positions of power and greatness. Many of us, long after the dreams of childhood and youth, nourish secret desires for power, wealth, and fame—to be a great athlete, musician, writer, singer, dancer, actor-actress, politician. We may secretly wish also to be loved deeply and intimately; to be taken care of; to be extricated from the web of existing relationships and responsibilities and to "start fresh and anew;" to be more spontaneous, more childlike with freedom to have fun in life.

A host of painful and sad secrets have to do with fears—fears of being rejected, disliked, even despised; of going crazy, committing suicide or dying; of being exposed as a fake; of being seen as inadequate, unattractive, ugly, utterly unlovable, or of never knowing

112

happiness. Sometimes we listen, sometimes we cannot, to our secrets that bring sadness, fear, and pain.

Secrets are commonly concerned with sex. Within the secrecy of our private world, sexual taboos lose much of their influence. We may allow ourselves to fantasize forbidden sexual pleasures. But related to our sexual secrets are also fears, conflicts, and guilt. Sexual secrets, therefore, may be regarded as dangerous, but also as marvelous and exciting avenues for power, love and intimacy.

The human body is a rich and manifold source of secret pleasures for those who can listen to their bodies and see them as beautiful, responsive to intimacy, and a marvel to experience. It is a source of pain, detraction, and irritation for those who are not attuned to their bodies and see them as ugly, weak, unfit, or simply as a necessity.

Looking back, some of us can remember secrets of the past, childhood secrets. Most are perhaps forgotten. Others, long since out in the open, hardly may be remembered as once having been a secret. Still others may now be memories. Secrets that through the years have become memories often have rich symbolic meaning, and revive both painful and happy experiences from the past.

Participants in my study remembered their secrets when younger as both good and bad. As they got older, their secrets became fewer and not so intense, not so frightening or uncontrollable. Important secrets became easier to handle. It became easier to decide whether or not to share, and easier to share or to withhold, once the decision was made.

As we get older our secrets are likely to become more deeply imbedded within us, more integrated within our behavior patterns and personality. Their influences may be more subtle. We may be less afraid of them and more willing and able to ferret them out. And we may listen to them more readily and acknowledge their meaning.

SECRETS AND POWER

We may enshroud another person with mystery because he knows or we imagine that he knows things that no one else does. Have you noticed that among children a secret may take on such significance in the eyes of playmates that if a child does not have one, he may act as if he does? If one child has a secret that he will not reveal, playmates soon may pretend to have an even bigger one. The pretense may maintain self-esteem, but it also establishes leverage for barter. "You tell me yours, and I'll tell you mine."

Exclusiveness in knowing may be associated with power on a grand scale. We may withhold as secret relatively unsecret information as a basis for exclusiveness, even elitism, for ourselves and a chosen few. The exclusiveness of the secret may take on more importance than its content. Withholding in secrecy has been known and practiced for centuries among politicians and government officials.[2] The political espionage in the infamous Watergate affair has underscored the dangers as well as the power in government secrecy. Such extreme secrecy usually reflects extreme greed for power.

Persons who have access to another's secrets have special influence. Access to secret information among lawyers, physicians, ministers, and psychotherapists constitutes power, of a sort, through the special privilege of knowing and not letting others know.

People who confide in psychotherapists and counselors may seek to endow them with power. But what might a person expect in return for his secrets? The therapist who reaches for power through probing to ferret out the patient's secrets and is so rewarded may be asked to pay up, to use what he now knows to give the patient solutions. The therapist may not be completely aware that such a barter with the patient is underway. Before the close of her first interview a woman patient was freely relating vivid details of recent sexual exploitations. She had not told this information to anyone before. Somewhat puzzled over such intimate confidences in the first interview, the male therapist finally interrupted to ask why she was sharing all this at this time. Her reply: "I am telling you everything so that you can straighten me out in a hurry." She, in effect, was seeking to trade her secrets for some kind of quick solution.

On the other hand, the person may confide in the therapist or some other listener to take away or lessen his or her power. And the therapist may unwittingly participate in such a barter. Several years ago a young woman spent most of our first interview telling me about past and current sexual activities. Near the end of the hour I questioned her about what this meant to her and what she wanted from talking about it in such a way. She smiled knowingly and replied, "I'm talking about it because I think it pleases you." Help! What was I doing? What cues might she be picking up that were secret from me, but seen by her? I had work to do in checking this out. My getting hooked into a barter in which the focus is on pleasing me through the sharing of sexual secrets will eliminate any impact I might have in the situation. I soon saw that what she told me, even though gamelike, was also a hint to listen carefully, to take her seriously, even though she might not take herself so, and not to get caught up in her stories that could keep us from gaining a deeper understanding of problems that were troubling her.

The therapist at times may not be certain that he even wants to know his patient's secrets. As a beginning therapist, I listened expectantly throughout three interviews anticipating that I would be told a deep, mysterious, and distressing secret by my young woman patient. My mind would race ahead to try to imagine things she might say. Would I be shocked? Could I remain calm? Would I be frightened and not know how to respond? My heart rate quickened. Was I too eager to hear? Or too afraid? Finally she let out what was bothering her. Her secret was: "I have no friends; other boys and girls do not like me. And I don't blame them. I'm worthless." What a letdown! After the patient's buildup and my corresponding expectations, I was ready to hear her confide something more like murder or incest.

I became painfully aware of my inadequacy in the situation. During the next interview I gathered courage to tell her that I was dissatisfied with my inability to be with her and that I had been listening both with fear and anticipation, not knowing whether or not I could accept what she might have to say. I also shared my desire to be able to listen to her, and at least to stay out of her way when she had something important to say. Immediately following my anxious confession, she replied simply and directly: "I feel sexually attracted to girls, and this really scares me. I don't understand it. I wanted to say it sooner, but for some reason couldn't get it out." One big reason: I was giving her both "go" and "stop" signals out of my need to know and my fear of knowing.

SECRETS AND FEAR

Sometimes what *we* fear most, either in ourselves or in others, may be seen by us as *their* secret. Have you ever feared the worst possibility upon going for a medical examination and then suspected that the physician was withholding a secret of your condition? And as a child, did you ever secretly suspect that your parents adopted you and withheld the truth? We can irrationally victimize ourselves with our own secrets and fears concerning secrets of others. Secrets can become an obsession. The person obsessed with secrecy may project so much intrigue and mystery onto the behavior of others that a simple gesture can no longer be taken at face value; rather it becomes a devious coverup for something hidden.

Have you suspected at times that there might be something secret about you that you do not even know yourself? Something too horrible to be allowed, too impossible to live with? Perhaps at other times it could be something rather nice if you could just listen to yourself and find out what it is. Or, it might be so vague that you have no idea how to go about listening to it. If it is there, it gets censored. Randy was perplexed because he was consistently late to the class he liked best. He told himself over and over again that he looked forward to this class, was fortunate to be taking it. Yet recently he had been as much as forty-five minutes late. He tried but could not find a reason. Not to know was unusual and frightening for him. With mounting anxiety he exclaimed: "It's the not knowing that really scares me now. It makes me wonder what else might be there." Later, looking back, Randy discovered how deeply afraid he was that something unknown and horrible about him might be revealed in this psychology class. He was afraid also that he would not use the opportunities class afforded to discover more about himself. The pull was powerful. He needed to be there, but he also needed to be late.

Speculating about what her unknown secrets might be in an early session of an intensive group experience, Rita wrote: "I was fascinated with what was shared. Such secrets that came out! They frightened me. Then I felt strangely hopeful. Like, 'maybe they can get me to

117

talk about things I don't know I want to talk about. Maybe they will be able to see through my façade and help me to talk about the things I really need to say. Wonder what they are?' It's hell even to think about what they might be!"

SECRETS AND SEPARATENESS

Our secrets may be the roots from which our individuality grows. Children discover special pleasure in knowing something secret and in using it to establish a domain of their own uniqueness. The child who finds that he knows things and does not have to tell his parents begins to discover his own separate identity and influence. He, like adults, may find satisfaction in simply knowing it. Or he may need to let others know that he has a secret and to find power in their knowing that he can keep it.

If a child is uneasy about what he knows, if having his secret leads him to feel tinged with guilt, he may not prize his uniqueness. He may give it up by telling. To expect him to share too many of his private experiences, especially when he prizes keeping some of them secret, may induce unnecessary and burdensome guilt. Prying into another's secrets also may encourage him to hide or withhold even unimportant details of his life. Parents who insist upon knowing all about their children's activities and thoughts may be distancing themselves from their children. Allowing a person, particularly in parent-child relationships, to have his or her secrets without undue curiosity or pressure to divulge them, can lead to closeness, comfort in knowing that the child, or parent, is free to share or not, and that either choice is acceptable.

A child is maturing and developing individuality when he has the ability to keep his own secrets. A later mark of development may be inferred from his ability to share voluntarily with another person, including his parents. Then he does not have to rebel by withholding everything to convince himself and others that he is gaining independence.[3] My son, when he was eleven, had an old copy of *Playboy* magazine in his room. Finally he placed it on his bookshelf where it could be seen. Nothing was said about his having it. One evening when I went to his room to tell him goodnight, he picked it up and began thumbing through it. Again, when no protest was made about his having the magazine, he offered it to me. He was through with it . . . at least for awhile.

As children and as adults our secrets bring privacy and strengthen our separateness. Without the ability to withhold some things, we may feel robbed of our separateness and individuality. Tricia, a young married woman of twenty-four, frequently announced during our counseling sessions, "I didn't know I knew that." She discovered with a mixture of relief and concern, "I always told everything to my mother and now I tell everything to my husband." Then, she complained, "And I'm beginning to feel cheated. Nothing I think or do is strictly my own."

With encouragement from her husband, Tricia began to withhold some of her thoughts and experiences to see how she felt about that. At first she felt guilt. Soon she began to enjoy it and to feel more, as she put it, "my own woman." She made a further discovery about why she kept finding out things in counseling that she never knew she knew. She said, "I could never afford to let myself have secrets. Because if I knew, I would have to tell. That's the way it's always been." Now Tricia was finding out that she did not have to tell everything. She was gaining the freedom to keep some things secret. She was gaining, therefore, more freedom to let *herself* know what she thought and felt. She began to lose the feeling that her mother and her husband were robbing her of her separateness.

Openness, sharing, and being together are enriched by the knowledge that parts of ourselves may remain secret, separate, not fully known to each other. Having secrets known clearly to ourselves, however, as a part of our separateness, adds to our autonomy and to what we have to offer each other in a relationship. We can share some of our secrets and retain some, thereby finding mutual satisfaction in the exchanges.

Barry Schwartz,[4] a sociologist, maintains that in social relationships acceptance of leaving-taking and actual separation are as important as time together. Being together is enhanced by physical separation as well as by separate psychological identities. I enjoy being with my family and close friends in especially joyful and sensitive ways following a period of separation. Similarly, being in deep, close relationships enhances time alone.

Relationships that are fairly stable can be strengthened, rather than endangered, by the establishment of privacy and interpersonal boundaries. Tricia's marriage was strengthened when she began to feel greater separateness from her husband. She could feel closer to him, and he found her more interesting and appealing.

I have talked about what our secrets often are like. They may be two-sided: happy, sad; light, heavy; friendly, antagonistic; comforting, frightening. Their content and significance are broad-ranging. They are sources of power, but also can bring impotence.

Learning how to keep some secrets is a part of growing up, a part of emotional maturity. Our secrets can be the roots of our individuality; they can help to define us as persons who are separate. At the same time they may enable us to be closer to one another, not more distant. Secrets, like sharing, can enrich our relationships.

Trouble may arise, however, when we try to determine which secrets to keep and which ones to reveal. Advance knowledge of the consequences of revealing or concealing ourselves may be hard to come by. Next I would like to explore ways we use our secrets for and against ourselves, alone and in relationships with other people.

10. The Secret Is You

The importance of secrets, in balance with self-revelation, has received little attention among social scientists and mental health practitioners. Self-disclosure, on the other hand, has been advocated extensively for psychological well-being. Perhaps its most articulate spokesman has been psychologist Sidney Jourard,[1] who also spearheaded much of the research on self-disclosure. Letting ourselves be known undoubtedly is important in establishing relationships, developing intimacy, and increasing self-understanding. Self-disclosure in itself, however, is not inevitably good. Research studies confirm what most of us probably know: that too little or too much self-revelation may be indicative of ineffective rather than effective personal functioning.

WHEN WE TELL TOO MUCH

Some sharing of our private worlds is essential for satisfying relationships and to avoid alienation. Indiscriminate self-revelation, however, like extreme isolation, also can lead to alienation. If I reveal myself willy-nilly, I am hard to get close to because no one knows what I represent as a person. Extreme self-disclosure may represent self-defeating behavior, for I may be out of control, unable to differentiate what I am expressing. I may experience catharsis, but I also may feel that others are distant from me. You, as the listener, may want to withdraw out of fear or disbelief.

Excessive openness may lead to the deception that we have no secrets, that we are what others see. Mowrer has aptly stated that "one's personality is, in truth, more importantly defined and structured by what is *un*known, inward, secret about him than by what is known."[2]

In therapy and some social groups, the continuous contact, desire for intimacy, and curiosity may result in a push for excessive self-revelation among members. Each person who reveals his weaknesses could be sharing his humanity, for to have problems is part of being human. But for a person to strip himself indiscriminately of his privacy, his secrets as it were, may not be humane or even in the best interests of that person or the group. Overexposure in a group climate may depersonalize, may rob the person of his individuality. Given a climate, however, where there is some protection and support for discrimination, a person may discover and decide for himself what to reveal and what to conceal. In learning to establish his own limits, he may discover also that this freedom brings greater trust in himself and others, greater spontaneity, and more genuineness. Such genuineness in what is revealed becomes more important than revealing everything about oneself indiscriminately.

Wholesale sharing of secrets in our lives is a form of defensiveness. I may develop a "defensive openness," that is, openness which is not genuine, as a way of presenting myself to you. If I open myself to you unselectively, you may see me as rootless, without boundaries, almost as a nonperson.

The behavior of Eloise, who was in her early thirties, will illustrate. Soon after I met her there seemed to be nothing about her personal life that she was unwilling to talk about. My first reaction was disbelief that words which ordinarily have personal private meaning and are expressed under special circumstances were flowing so freely. Then I noticed that the words did not carry the emotional tones of privacy. It was as though she were walking naked down the street, but acting as though she were fully clothed, utterly lacking in self-consciousness.

Unlike the person who confides indiscreetly to shock or to burden another person, Eloise shared herself excessively for other reasons. She was out of touch with herself and unable to determine what was appropriate to say to whom. Her self-picture was ill-defined, fluid—like spilled liquid, spreading too fast too far. She had difficulty in establishing bonds of intimacy with other people. She shared the ingredients of intimacy, but they lacked authenticity. Associates could not find her in her disclosures and, consequently, could not make contact with her as a separate individual.

Learning what to share, when to share, and with whom, like learning how to keep some secrets truly secret, is a part of psychological growth. The way we keep and share our secrets is rooted in deeper facets of our personality. Such was the case with Eloise, who failed to develop a satisfactory inner definition of her individuality.

WHICH SECRETS TO TELL, WHAT TO EXPECT?

Recently I recalled an essay by Hobart Mowrer[3] in which he relates a story from the novel *Magnificent Obsession* by Lloyd C. Douglas. In the story Dr. Wayne Hudson became a famous brain surgeon by applying a secret he learned from a talented sculptor. I read *Magnificent Obsession* and found that Dr. Hudson performed great deeds, particularly gifts of philanthropy, with the understanding that his deeds would be kept secret while he was alive. From his secret acts he gained self-esteem, perhaps a certain nobility in his own eyes and the eyes of those he served. As a consequence he became energized, brilliantly effective, and transcended his earlier more ordinary life. The formula was: keep secret the good deeds and save the credit as something of value, rather than tell them and thereby spend the credit.

Professor Mowrer in his essay advocates keeping the secrets of the good, but takes another step in advocating giving away the bad secrets by confessing them. Mowrer writes: "Most of us live depleted existences: weak, zestless, apprehensive, pessimistic, 'neurotic.' And the reason is that when we perform a *good deed*, we advertise it, display it—and thus collect and enjoy the credit then and there. But when we do something cheap and mean, we carefully hide and deny it (if we can), with the result that the 'credit' for acts of *this* kind remains with us and 'accumulates.' A person who follows such a life-style is chronically bankrupt in the moral and spiritual sense. If, at any given moment, his life were 'required of him,' he would be found *wanting*, could not pay out, settle up; for his 'net worth' is less than nothing, negative. Small wonder, then, that a person of this kind has no confidence or zest and lacks creativity. He is too busy pretending, too 'insecure,' too afraid of being 'found out.' "[4] Mowrer's solution: "confession of past misdeeds and . . . concealment of future 'good works.' "[5]

Which secrets should be told? The good? The bad? None? It may be exceedingly easy or difficult for some of us to decide which ones to tell, which ones to keep. If they are burdensome, sharing them may bring relief, or be a step toward it. Other secrets may be simply too exciting not to let someone we trust and like in on them. And a few secrets may need to be told with the proper touch of artfulness so that they will be retold by others.

On the other side, a secret may be too damaging to tell, at least immediately. The cost of telling could be higher than the cost of keeping the secret. Then again, telling some secrets might constitute a breach of confidence.

We usually stand to gain or to lose something either in telling or keeping our secrets. We can weigh the temptation of revealing or of concealing a particular secret against the possibilities of hurt or enhancement, for ourselves and others, but seldom can we know with certainty the consequences in advance.

What might be expected if an important secret is shared with a friend? Participants in my study of secrets were inclined to expect feelings of relief, reassurance, understanding, acceptance, a special feeling of closeness, and sometimes reciprocity—"I've told you mine, now you tell me yours." Still, they would rather listen to the secrets of friends than to risk telling their own. Generally speaking, they saw themselves as being more open and more giving to others than they expected others to be to them. What they expected to give, however, was essentially the same as what they expected to receive. Upon hearing the secrets of others they expected to feel interested, trusted, privileged, warm, close, and influential.

One pervasive concern: can others listen, understand, give support, and be trusted to keep our secrets? Many of us do have difficulty keeping secrets that others share with us. It is not surprising that we should suspect them of having the same problem. But we also may see ourselves as interested, open, and accepting of the secrets of others, while suspecting that they will regard our secrets as "silly," "trivial," "shocking," "perverse," or "overwhelming."

Are we more considerate of others than of ourselves? Perhaps. Then again, the stakes are higher when we tell our secrets than when we listen to those of others. We may have little to lose in our openness to the secrets of others, but much to lose in making the wrong predictions about their openness to ours.

The implications of keeping or telling some secrets are by no means simple. Neither are the outcomes entirely predictable in many of our relationships. For instance, feelings of guilt that accompany withholding of a secret may bring about different reactions. Jim felt guilty for having lunch with a former girlfriend, but did not share it with his wife, Ellen. As a result he became more considerate and kinder with the intent of making it up to her. The relationship seemed closer during that time. Ellen reacted differently to her secret. She felt guilty for buying new clothes with money she had earned and for telling Jim that her mother paid for them. She wanted the clothes very much, but had a nagging feeling that the money was needed more for household items. Rather than compensate for her guilt by being extra nice, as Jim did, she resented it and displaced her resentment on Jim by being impatient and short-tempered with him for days.

Similarly, confession of secrets may affect relationships in unpredictable ways. If I confess my secret misdeed you might mistrust my representation of myself to you in the future. Or you might accept my confession as evidence that I am trustworthy, though perhaps sometimes misguided. Then again, even if you want to forgive me you might instead act in ways that punish me and strain our relationship because you feel betrayed and have taken my misdeed as a personal affront.

The consequence of having revealed a secret may build up new tensions not easily dissolved. By confessing behavior that we seek to change, for example, we may reinforce in the eyes of others a stereotype of that behavior. As a consequence, the behavior may become more encased in the mold we are trying to break. Let me illustrate how such a possibility was faced. In his second group therapy session, Rich, showing tension through body movements and tone of voice, looked around the room at the other members and said, "There is something I would like to tell about me." He glanced nervously around the room again and then at the therapist. He was feeling conflict over whether or not to tell his secret. From an earlier individual session the therapist could guess what it was. Were the situation and his secret ripe for the telling?

Having met together only once before, the group members were still relative strangers. There was little basis for trust in the group at this point, but members' taking the risk to share is a step toward building needed trust. Would Rich stand to gain or lose in his own eyes, in the eyes of other group members, and in terms of his prospects for growth? The therapist's hunch at that moment was that Rich was setting himself up to be misunderstood, for superficial acceptance, or perhaps rejection, any or all of which could diminish his own sagging self-esteem. The therapist responded, "I would like to suggest that you wait two or three sessions and then tell us if you still want to. What is your reaction to that?"

Rich's facial expression and body posture conveyed feelings of both disappointment and relief. He replied, however, "Okay, I'll do that." Now he appeared let down, more disappointed than relieved.

Rich never revealed his secret in the group. He did reveal some related problems on which he could work. His secret was that he had been involved in an active sexual relationship with another man. Now he was growing dissatisfied with this relationship and wanted to work on developing satisfying heterosexual relationships.

Months later he expressed to the therapist his reaction to that second session and subsequent developments. "That was a turning point for me. I was really down, depressed, and lonely, going through some bad times trying to get over this unsatisfactory sexual relationship. I felt that if I opened up that part of my life to the group, maybe they could help. In retrospect my motive might have been to elicit sympathy. I did a lot of that during that period of my life. But my attempt at bringing this up fell through; I never told my secret and so I did not collect much sympathy. And for a while I was really mad at you. I thought you had cut me off and made me go a different direction.

"And now I think back in horror at the way it could have gone and am glad you questioned my telling the group. Later it dawned on me that I was not a puppet. After months of self-pity and unhappiness with myself and the world, I finally began enjoying things and people, and felt like a new person. I am just beginning to accept the fact that there is substance to me and that many people like and some even envy me. I sometimes turn to friends for help when there are moments of absolute desperation. But, in general, I feel more in control of my fate. It's truly a neat feeling."

129

By keeping his secret, Rich helped himself get a different perspective on his life, including his sexual behavior. He also kept others from the possibility of reinforcing his self-pity and a life style he wanted to try to change.

BONDS OR BURDENS?

A secret between us may become an emotional tie that brings us together or a burdensome obstacle that keeps us apart. My intent in telling my secret may be to give a part of myself, a gift. I may share some secrets to find relief, to diminish or change my feelings about the secret. I might share other secrets as a bid for friendship, possibly intimacy, through mutual sharing. Privately shared hardships and adversity endured can bring us closer. When a member of an intensive therapy group shares a long-held, important secret, the participants may feel deeply the trust placed in them. They may value the person who shared for having faith in them. Members often feel an extraordinary bond of intimacy, particularly if the secret involves pain and suffering. Sharing becomes even more poignant if the secret represents a present experience rather than an incident out of the past. In the experience with Ted, described in the last chapter on silences, a bond of intimacy was felt among group members who accompanied him on his journey into his secret fear of isolation.

Incidents long past that remain secrets may still have impact, if there is sufficient emotional involvement or risk in the present telling. The goal in emotionally charged or high-risk sharing is not intimacy or close ties to another, but reduction of suffering and resolution of conflict. Intimacy becomes a salient by-product. A secret shared by Sharon, a single woman in her early twenties, is an example.

130

During the first few group sessions, Sharon had talked only a few times, and then briefly, about her shyness in social situations and minor conflicts with her parents over her plans to enter law school. She appeared to be greatly interested, however, in the concerns other members explored. During the sixth session, Mike, recently divorced, mentioned that he missed his three children so much that he had begun to dream about them at night. Sharon burst into tears and seemed instantly overcome with grief. Flashes of surprise, along with concern, were reflected on the faces of some of the other members. Within a few minutes Sharon regained sufficient composure to talk.

"For weeks," she said, "I've been wanting to talk about something that I have been thinking about constantly. It's haunting me, and I'm scared to death when I wonder what's happening to me." She hesitated to hold back a rush of tears.

"Each time I get ready to talk about it, I get even more scared, or I begin to think it's not really important. Then when Mike said how much he missed his children, I couldn't hold back any longer." Again Sharon stopped to get control of her emotions. Others were now absorbed in what she was saying.

She began again. "Four years ago, when I was seventeen, I had a baby girl. After six weeks of agonizing and many, many tears, I decided to give her up for adoption. My parents supported me in the decision. I have not seen or heard about her since. Most of the time I feel like the decision was the right one. Even now it seems right." Sharon was more in control now, and spoke with less hesitation.

"But the past two months have been strange for me. I have been thinking about her, wondering what she is like now that she is four. I wonder what she will think about me when she grows up . . . or if she will even know that I am her mother. That's when I feel sad."

131

Tears came again, but she continued. "What's strange is that I know I made the right decision, and yet I feel so terribly sad." She sat quietly for a moment. "I just plain miss her . . . and I even want her to miss me too." Sharon stopped talking and cried softly. Muted sobs could be heard in the room. Several members were sitting close by, listening quietly.

"Yes, I really do miss her, and saying it out loud right now somehow makes it more okay." She looked at others close by and continued, as though talking mostly to herself. "Maybe it's not so strange for me to think about her and to miss her." Nods of approval and support from others were evident; some were crying still. With this last statement, giving herself permission to feel sadness again over the loss of her daughter, Sharon became more relaxed and brighter. So did the expressions of others who, in their support and quiet caring, had joined her in this poignantly shared experience. No words or physical signs were needed for us to know that this was a moment of closeness to Sharon and to one another. Her hurt and sadness of some four years ago was reawakened in the present for all of us.

Secrets may bind and at the same time separate us in unhappy and hurtful ways. The threat that you might reveal our secret and cause me harm may bind me in fear. But the threat also may lead me to feel estranged and distrusting. Actual revelation of a potentially damaging secret may cause the persons involved to resent that the secret exists, and also to resent one another.

Occasionally the person who shares his secret expects to be admonished or punished. Usually, however, when punishment or other negative consequences are expected, the secret is kept, unless the pain of keeping it is too great. Still, there are times when a person may share his secret to be seen as bad, to get reactions that will fire up his anger or that will feed his belief that he is worthless. But other people need not necessarily be involved for us to feel the gravity of our secrets.

Some secret fears sap our vitality; secret guilt shrinks our self-esteem. And secrets that embody hopelessness when no relief is in sight leave us in despair. We can use our secrets, moreover, as potentially destructive forms of self-blackmail. I may conceal a secret and repeatedly remind myself reproachfully of its badness, using the process as a weapon of control, a constant reminder for the future. A secret may be confessed, not for relief and freedom, but in payment for a deplorable act. Having paid by suffering the humiliation of confession, I may tell myself that I will never behave in such a way again.

Either concealment or confession may become forms of self-extortion and, therefore, become self-defeating. They signal that I have not come to terms with my secret acts, have not integrated them as a part of myself, even though they are in the past. I am still striving to keep them outside, apart from me.

When we share a secret that is worrisome and expect the other person to take over and absorb our worries, we may be seeking in still another way to cast off a part of ourselves that we wish to disclaim. Unless we can come to terms with our secrets and claim them as our own, whether they represent joy or despair, we are likely to have difficulty disposing of them, whether as gifts, as pawns, as yokes.

We may need to share a secret but have difficulty letting go, letting someone else know what it means to us. Katherine, in her early twenties and married a year, believed for as long as she could remember that she would die young. Recently, the thought of early death gripped her with fear. She felt guilty and deceptive for not sharing her fear with Frank, her husband. She needed to confront her fear and to tell Frank. In the second therapy session she imagined herself telling Frank. In her fantasy she said to herself and to Frank, "I feel afraid again. I want to laugh and say, 'Oh, never mind,' to break the tension. He is sitting there expectantly. I have his full attention. My mind darts ahead ... I wonder, how will you react? Will you laugh or say, 'Is that all?' or make light of it? I don't feel any doubts about whether you will keep my secret. I know it is safe with you. What I worry about is how you will react to it. What if you think it is silly—no, not silly, just unimportant or not that big a deal. That reaction from you would hurt so much."

A day later Katherine made an abortive attempt to tell Frank. She began much like she did in her fantasy, with nervous laughter to break the tension as though it were just something silly on her mind. As a result, Frank did not understand the gripping fear of Katherine's secret. After further work she set out to tell him again. This time she let it out as she felt it, neither minimizing nor exaggerating. Frank sensed her fear and felt its power. From that moment its importance for Katherine began to fade.

To know the secret anguish of someone we love may cause us grief. The deeper our love for another person the more vulnerable we are to suffering the pain of his or her hurts, humiliations, and failures. For this reason we sometimes have spoken and unspoken agreements not to share some of our secrets. We need the freedom for such agreements. But we also need agreements to share and to suffer with one another if our compassion and ability to care are to be kept alive.

SECRETS AND NONSECRETS SWITCH

Other people greatly influence what we regard as secret and not secret. Our secrets and disclosures are likely to be different with our attorney, our minister, our physician, and our best friend. What constitutes secrets and what becomes shared within a family change over time, just as secrets and nonsecrets are in flux in other relationships. We may not need to hold secret now what we earlier considered secret.

When our younger daughter was six, we decided that it was time to tell the identity of Santa Claus. It turned out that she had somehow discovered the secret two years earlier. She had kept her knowledge of it as her own secret in order not to risk losing out on a good thing.

Emily, a young woman in therapy, was in a quandary. She was falling in love with Jack, who was an eligible prospect for marriage. When should she tell him that she could never have children? She might have been presumptuous to tell him earlier. Now she might have waited too long. How would Jack react? She decided to tell him and risk being rejected and hurt. Jack was deeply disappointed and saddened, both for her and himself. But he cared very much for Emily and, through her sharing, he was able to tell her his feelings. Emily felt great relief.

Legal sanctions and prohibitions, social customs, popular attitudes, and a myriad of other influences operate to switch secrets to disclosures and vice versa. A few years ago the woman who did not want children most likely kept her secret. Today the desire to have a large family may be kept as secret by some couples. Mary Anne found herself wanting to keep her pregnancy a secret from her young friends who were concerned with problems of overpopulation. Mary Anne had two children already.

The use of alcohol has remained public knowledge in some communities, but secret in others. Stories old and new, apocryphal and true, still circulate about members of conservative religious groups who steal secretly to the "back door" for a drink while their more liberal neighbors go through the front. Persuasive advertising made cigarette smoking by women virtually a social amenity. As pressures continue to mount against cigarette smoking as a health hazard, smokers may find themselves wanting to smoke in secret more than in public.

What was once secret may now be open badges for acceptance, for membership in the group. Tommy's crowd of teenagers was experimenting with marijuana. His secret was that he had never tried it and did not want to. Finally he risked open rejection by telling his group. They made an exception; he could still be one of them. Some college students in the late sixties were selective in revealing their ambitions for high-status professional, executive positions, and for wealth and material luxury. They were less secretive about wanting to be leisurely, loaf, or travel—what we used to call "bum around the world" for awhile. Today they find more acceptance among peers for feeling ambitious professionally and in the job market.

As attitudes toward sex and sexual behavior become more open what will become secret? The fact that one has not experimented much with numerous sexual partners? Desire for sexual fidelity? If a young college woman wants to get married and devote most of her time to being a wife and mother, she may not feel free to acknowledge this desire openly. At a party, Carol, who was finishing her Ph.D. and planning a career in psychology, asked Janet what she planned to do after she got married. Janet exchanged sheepish looks with her fiancé and replied with noticeable embarrassment, "I just want to be a wife and mother." Carol, now embarrassed, found herself in the "ridiculous position" of assuring Janet that she didn't think that was so bad, and that she shouldn't be ashamed of it. With changes in male and female sex roles in our culture, more men may be relatively free to acknowledge that they would like to be supported financially by their girlfriends or wives.

There is conspicuous evidence that openness is increasing among young people and large numbers of older adults, and that many things once secret are secret no longer. There are also signs which tell us that as we change what we are open about, we also are changing what we are secret about. If we listen carefully to ourselves and sort out which among our secrets and disclosures have switched, we may find that we still have a balance between the two, a balance that serves our own particular emotional balance and patterns of behavior. Some of us will continue to withhold more of our secrets. Others will continue to share more. Each of us expects a variety of payoffs—whether we get them or not—from what we share and what we withhold.

WE ARE OUR SECRETS

Theodor Reik, who talks about Sigmund Freud's tenacious search for the secrets of human behavior, tells the story of the bold young man of Sais, which was "for some time the capital of ancient lower Egypt and the seat of her wisest priests. The saga reports that there was a mysterious veiled statue, the figure of Truth, in one of the magnificent temples of Sais. It was strictly forbidden to unveil the sacred image. A daring youth once tore the cover from the statue, as the poet tells us:

> But one succeeded in raising the veil,
> And he saw—wonder of wonder!—himself." [6]

We are our secrets, just as we are what we reveal for others to hear and to see. Our secrets shape us, just as responses from others influence us. There can be both beauty and fear in the realization that there is no end to the process of discovering secret facets of ourselves.

All of us harbor within us mystery, surprises, and the capacity to hide, to seek, and to change—unless we have gotten so much out of touch with life that we have become emotionally moribund. All of us hold rich veins of both strikingly unique and somewhat ordinary secrets about what it is like to be human.

Notes

Chapter 1

1. Cornelis B. Bakker, "Why People Don't Change," *Psychotherapy: Theory, Research and Practice* 12, no. 2 (1975): 164–72.
2. Ibid.

Chapter 7

1. Carl R. Rogers, *Client Centered Therapy* (New York: Houghton Mifflin, 1951), p. ix.
2. R. P. Blackmur, "The Language of Silence," in R. N. Anshen, ed., *Language: An Inquiry into Its Meaning and Function* (New York: Harper, 1957), p. 152.
3. Theodor Reik, *Listening with the Third Ear* (Garden City, N.Y.: Garden City Books, 1948), p. 125.
4 Ibid., p. 24.

Chapter 8

1. "Hello Walls" (BMI), sung by Willie Nelson, recorded by RCA Records (ACI–1326 Stereo) Camden, New York, N.Y., 1973.
2 Viktor Frankl, *Man's Search for Meaning* (New York: Washington Square Press, 1959), pp. 109–110.
3 Theodor Reik, *Listening with the Third Ear* (Garden City, N.Y.: Garden City Books, 1948), p. 123.
4. Frieda Fromm-Reichmann, "Loneliness," in W. G. Bennis et al., eds., *Interpersonal Dynamics* (Homewood, Ill.: Dorsey Press, 1968), pp. 121–38.
5. Ibid., pp. 133–36.
6. Frankl, *Man's Search for Meaning*, pp. 139–40.

Chapter 9

1. For this study I prepared a series of 48 incomplete sentences (called stems) on secrets, written so that each person could fill in his own individual responses. Participants did not sign their names. Slightly over half of the 80 persons completing the sentences were women; slightly over half were married. Ages ranged from 20 to 46; the average age was a little over 30.
2. *The Sociology of George Simmel*, ed. and trans. Kurt H. Wolff (Glencoe, Ill.: Free Press, 1950), part 4.
3. Paul Tournier, *Secrets*, trans. Joe Embry (Richmond, Va.: John Knox Press, 1965), p. 29.
4. Barry Schwartz, "The Social Psychology of Privacy," *American Journal of Sociology 73* (May 1968): 741–52.

Chapter 10

1. Sidney M. Jourard, *Transparent Self* (Princeton, N.J.: D. Van Nostrand, 1964) and *Disclosing Man to Himself* (Princeton, N.J.: D. Van Nostrand, 1968).
2. O. Hobart Mowrer, *The New Group Therapy* (Princeton, N.J.: D. Van Nostrand, 1964), p. 70.
3. Ibid.
4. Ibid., p. 66.
5. Ibid., p. 68
6. Theodor Reik, *The Secret Self* (New York: Grove Press, 1952), pp. 8–9.